Praise for *Empowered, Sexy, and Free*

"Sisters! This book is bound to take you on an expansive journey of self-discovery and remembrance of who you truly are. Jolie Dawn embodies what she teaches and shows other women how to create a life that they are in love with by using the practical and actionable tools in this book."

— AMANDA GOOLSBY, speaker, facilitator,
and spiritual business advisor

"Jolie Dawn is an extraordinary author, one who truly helps women capture their brilliance and step into new possibilities. If you have forgotten who you came to this world to be, this book will help you remember."

— JACKI BEEM, founder of Hi-Watt Living

"*Empowered, Sexy, and Free* is like having direct access to both a private coach and a big sister who empowers you to bloom into the best version of you. Jolie Dawn lets no one, as challenged as they might feel with their life's circumstances, get stuck into thinking they don't have the power to create their life with more abundance and joy. Read this book if you dare to unlock the magic you have within and to live your desires as your reality."

— ALLIE MCFEE, women's health educator with
Modern Goddess Lifestyle

"Every woman must know the power of living the kind of life Jolie Dawn describes as 'empowered, sexy, and free.' This book is truly a must-have road map for the modern woman for how to embody the new paradigm for living a wildly successful, turned-on, and purposeful life."

— JULES SCHROEDER, founder of Unconventional Life

"Jolie Dawn has the gift of writing; her words become ours. Her book guides you from immaturity to wisdom. Jolie's is the voice of the big sister, elder, and mentor my youthful self always wished for. There is nothing like a good book that paints the picture of a youthful broken woman transformed into a wise, enlightened one. May this book shorten your journey to the best parts of you."

— DEBRA SILVERMAN, psychotherapist and founder of Applied Astrology

"Have you ever contemplated just what it would take to enrich and electrify your life, while making a huge impact on others? Jolie Dawn has laid out a decadent spread of juicy, delicious possibilities that every woman should consider as she creates her journey through this lifetime. And, powerfully, Jolie shows you how to actualize fulfillment and satisfaction with powerful tools I've witnessed her using firsthand to magically create a 'hell yes' life! I couldn't put this down!"

— MISTY WILLIAMS, founder of Healing Rosie

"*Empowered, Sexy, and Free* is a delight for the soul. Jolie Dawn nourishes us with her ability to sweetly illustrate a woman's journey home to herself. Any woman ready to be deeply seen and powerfully inspired will greatly benefit from picking up this book."

— NINA CAMILLE, creator of Experience Freedom and coauthor of *The Empowered Woman Series, Book 2*

"An empowering book for women, reminding us that the radical power we hold is a gift to the world and is meant to be shared. Jolie, thank you for seeing women so deeply and intimately, and for lovingly guiding us through the beauty of your words."

— TAMEIKA GENTLES, cofounder of The Whole Experience Inc.

"Profound, crystal clear, and epically transformative. I felt deep shifts and cried lots of tears even in the first few pages. I'm eternally grateful this book exists — for me and for women everywhere. Jolie, thank you for sharing your magic to inspire our own."

— DR. KATHERINE M. ZAGONE, naturopathic doctor

EMPOWERED *Sexy* AND FREE

EMPOWERED Sexy AND FREE

Discover Your Unique Brilliance and
Dare to Be the Creatrix of Your Life

JOLIE DAWN

New World Library
Novato, California

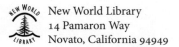 New World Library
14 Pamaron Way
Novato, California 94949

The material in this book is intended for education. It is not meant to take the place of diagnosis and treatment by a qualified medical practitioner or therapist. No expressed or implied guarantee of the effects of the use of the recommendations can be given or liability taken.

Text design by Tona Pearce Myers

Library of Congress Cataloging-in-Publication Data

Names: Dawn, Jolie, author.
Title: Empowered, sexy, and free : discover your unique brilliance and dare to
    be the creatrix of your life / Jolie Dawn.
Description: Novato, California : New World Library, [2022] | Summary: "A
    fresh and irreverent take on living well, based not on changing you but on
    fully being you"-- Provided by publisher.
Identifiers: LCCN 2021049900 (print) | LCCN 2021049901 (ebook) | ISBN
    9781608686643 (paperback) | ISBN 9781608686650 (epub)
Subjects: LCSH: Self-actualization (Psychology) | Change (Psychology) |
    Self-confidence.
Classification: LCC BF637.S4 D386 2022 (print) | LCC BF637.S4 (ebook) |
    DDC 158.1--dc23/eng/20211119
LC record available at https://lccn.loc.gov/2021049900
LC ebook record available at https://lccn.loc.gov/2021049901

Parts of the book appeared in a previous edition published by the author.
First printing, February 2022
ISBN 978-1-60868-664-3
Ebook ISBN 978-1-60868-665-0
Printed in the USA on 100% postconsumer-waste recycled paper

 New World Library is proud to be a Gold Certified Environmentally
Responsible Publisher. Publisher certification awarded by Green Press
Initiative.

10   9   8   7   6   5   4   3   2   1

I dedicate this book to my mom, Lynn, for passing to me the love of writing and creative self-expression. Mom, your human self would have felt all kinds of ways about the revealing stories about our relationship in this book, but I know your spirit is beside me in full support, cheering me on, cheering us on. Thank you for being my guardian angel. I feel you always. I love you always.

Contents

Introduction

Welcome, sister. I am so happy that you are here. We may not know each other intimately, but we come from the same place. My soul recognizes your soul. My heart is happy that you are taking this journey for yourself. Welcome to the first day of the rest of your life.

You're here because you want a life that totally turns you on. You want to be empowered, sexy, and free. What does that life actually look like?

To me, it looks like being so confident in yourself that you light up a room when you enter. No more dimming your light just so others feel comfortable around you.

It looks like waking up each morning feeling peace, a sense of direction, and absolute joy for being alive. Goodbye to waking up feeling rushed, anxious, and burned out.

It looks like leaving behind the world of comparison, jealousy, and competition. Instead, you enter into a new paradigm of genuine happiness for others who are succeeding on their journeys. You no longer perceive them as threats. Their existence creates a real feeling of joy and affirmation for you, secure in your knowledge that this reality is a beautiful place with room for all to ascend and succeed.

It looks like living in what I call "remembrance." A woman in remembrance knows who she is, where she came from, and why she is here on this wild journey we call "the human experience." It's when you are uniquely yourself, daring to be an individual, radiating your inner light, and expanding the heart of every human who is a witness to your divine feminine essence.

It may also look like having a career that you love, random and frequent miracles, a beautiful practice of self-love, rich friendships and connections, love and peace in your family, an abundance of money and other resources, a healthy and strong body, and a clear understanding of your strengths and unique brilliance.

Sounds pretty amazing, right?

Let me start by reminding you of a simple, undeniable truth: *You are already a masterpiece.* You were born as nothing short of a divine mirror image of God. From the moment you took your first breath to the exact moment you're in now, your life is a true miracle and something to be revered. Would you believe me if I told you that you already have everything you could ever want *inside* you? You may not feel that in this current moment, and that's okay. The most brilliant, alive you may be temporarily covered by energetic weight that you have been carrying, weight that served you at some point as an adaptation to life but no longer benefits you. This book will guide you through a process of removing that energetic weight so you can access the purpose and manifestation superpowers you already possess.

This weight that we will release together shows up in life

as little bits of resistance and triggers: drama in relationships, tension with your partner, money scarcity, a job you are bored with, a business that is testing your sanity, friends who don't reciprocate the same degree of love you give, days of stress and anxiety, a feeling of disconnection and isolation, and whatever else may be repeatedly taking you from your joy, inner peace, and aliveness. Does any of this sound familiar?

Full disclosure: This process won't necessarily be comfortable. It can be a very scary feeling to shake up your current reality and your current belief systems. Your ego will be alarmed and may tell you that you are not safe. Your friends may think you've gone a little nuts. I encourage you to stay with the process, even when you're feeling confronted and want to run. Truly, everything that you want for yourself is on the other side of your fear. And as each layer of energetic weight gets dissolved and stripped away, you will realize how empowered, sexy, and free you are right now, in this very moment. With this newfound lightness and sense of personal power, you have the opportunity to become a creatrix like never before: the version of you that creates her desired reality on command. This version of you is waiting to be claimed. Do you dare?

We've all heard motivational speakers say, "You have a gift that no one else has, you are special, blah blah blah." These words are nice and give us moments of inspiration, but their power is short-lived. Why? Because we don't really believe them. We believe the lie that hundreds of other women have gifts more powerful than ours. We have endless confirmations that thousands of other women have better lives than ours. We see them on social media every single day. The fitness babe with the perfect bikini body, the woman who is crushing multi-five-figure months in her business, the seemingly ideal boyfriend who just proposed to her with your dream ring, or the wild spirit who is traveling to all of your bucket list places. It can be so damn triggering at times, huh? Especially on an extra sensitive day.

Sister, it's time to make *your* life the life you most want to live. *Your* body is your favorite, *your* life is the most inspiring, *your* real life experiences captured in your photos are the most exciting scrolling material. What would it take to be *that* in love with yourself and the life you've created? It's time to put intentional effort into introspection and to be relentless in discovering the vast gifts that lay fully or partially dormant inside you. I promise you, they are so much bigger and brighter than you could ever imagine.

This book is your guide into a deeply introspective place. Whether this is your first time diving deep inside or you are a seasoned seeker, you will find endless diamonds of truth hidden inside you. I am not simply going to tell you that you are unique and special. I am going to *show* you so that you know this to be the ultimate truth. Because when you remember this truth, your entire world changes in the best ways. It's as if your garden just sprouted flowers in the most brilliant shades and the trees are bursting with life-giving fruits where before there were weeds and dry patches. It's up to you to plant the seeds, that's your choice.

Every single tool and practice I've written in this book has come from my own firsthand experience. Everything I share with you here is what I use on a daily basis to create and maintain a life that I absolutely adore and how I come home to myself when it all feels hard and messy. I'm here to pass on to you what has worked for me to sustain an empowered, sexy, and free life.

My stories are raw and real because speaking my truth always sets me free. I share in this way so you may have the courage to share your truth as well. Shame can only live in the dark; the light of truth is the way back to light.

One word that kept running through my mind as I was writing was *digestibility*. My goal is to make it easy for you to digest and understand the content in this book and just as easy to use it to take action in your life. I've read books before that were highly inspiring but didn't end up actually making a difference in my life. This book is an action-packed manual with an intention of helping you achieve practical transformation.

I invite you to take what you learn here and play with it in real life; I will guide you in doing so throughout each chapter. Like anything in life, the more effort you put in, the more rewards you will get out. So let me ask you now: How would you like to play? As an observer standing outside the garden fence, peeking in? Or alongside me in the garden, hands in the dirt, planting the seeds of your gorgeous future, playing full out, knowing that our time here on planet Earth is precious and limited? The choice is yours.

Yes, I've been a seeker on a spiritual path for years, worked with clients all over the world, hosted conferences, spoken on stages, and had thousands of hours of transformational training. But I am not pretending to be a guru, an enlightened master, or someone who has it all figured out. I'm simply here to share what has worked for me and what I believe will be helpful for you. If anything I say feels right and light for you, keep it. If it feels wrong or heavy, throw it out. You call the shots. Your truth wins.

So the real questions are: Are you *willing* to have the life you want? Are you willing to access new realms of peace and joy, to be a carrier of light in the world, to maximize your pleasure in every moment? To be a captivating woman with the life force of her spirit beaming through her eyes? Are you willing to let go of being the victim, let go of energetic weight, and discover your unique brilliance? Do you dare to turn on your creatrix superpowers?

Right here, right now, take a look at your arms and hands. Your legs and feet. Your beautiful torso (yes, it *is*). Your miraculous face. Right now, open your camera on your phone and look at that face. Let your heart fill up with love for everything you've been through and how well you've survived (yes, you *have*). Speak out loud: "My name is _____." Say your name and hear your voice. Allow yourself to be delighted by the sound of your own name.

You have been given this one body in this lifetime. Your perfectly crafted physical form, your brilliant personality, your beautiful voice, your essence — it's all right here on planet Earth for but a blink of an eye in the vast timeline of human history. You are everything and nothing, all in one. A speck of dust among the billions of stars. Your life is so significant and so insignificant at the same time. Your ability to accept paradoxes in this reality will save you much time and heartache.

You've been given the chance in this incarnation to understand yourself, awaken to your power, embrace your sexuality, claim your freedom, achieve your healing, and do what you came here to do, your "dharma" or soul's purpose. Every day you are building your legacy. What will it be? Let's find out.

Who Am I to Have the Privilege to Guide You?

Who am I to offer you an invitation to walk the path toward becoming empowered, sexy, and free? Let me tell you who.

I'm a sensitive woman who has watched people I loved take their dreams to their graves and has realized how precious and short life is.

I'm a caring friend who grieved when one of my best friends committed suicide because she felt worthless in this world.

I'm an entrepreneur who discovered how to support my life and future in abundance by making it up as I went along, by having a big heart to serve others, and by following my desire to create the world I want to live in.

I'm an irreverent, wild spirit who dared to challenge the norms of society and live my wild, untamed, crazy truth.

I'm a sexual, sensual woman who struggled for decades with sexual repression and internalized shame, who embraced my greatest fears of rejection, and who allowed myself to have the love I always wanted.

I'm a businesswoman who launched projects before I felt ready — as I was scared shitless, in fact — and has repeatedly created multi-six-figure online launches with my tenacity and resourcefulness.

I'm a novice, never-trained writer who finished my first book in three months, self-published, and hit the Amazon bestseller list in the most competitive categories, like spirituality and women in business, next to the most prolific *New York Times* bestselling authors of our time. I dared to publish before I was ready, then sat back as thousands of people around the world read my book and hundreds of reviews and messages poured in — messages of gratitude and resonance.

I'm a girl's girl, a lover of the feminine spirit in every way, and a catalyst for the awakening of women all around me.

I am a woman with a dream, like you. I am every woman

and only this one unique woman. I have suffered and felt intense pain, and I have experienced deep joy and ecstasy. Every day I find something new to love about this life. I am writing the story of my legacy every. Single. Day.

I'm a woman who spent years denying my power and decades suffering from trauma I didn't know how to resolve, let alone know that it was even possible to resolve. If there was one thing I knew how to do really well for years, it was to pretend. I pretended that I loved myself, that everything was okay, that my family life was fine, that I was happy. But just underneath the surface, I was a hot mess. I was making choices that hurt my body and my well-being, and I couldn't seem to stop. The pain and shame inside me felt so big, and I was so terrified to look at it, that I unconsciously sought comfort in all the most destructive ways.

I discovered alcohol at fourteen. I absolutely loved how I felt when I was drunk: carefree, sexy, desired, and uninhibited. Thus began my ten-year love affair with alcohol. Most weekends in high school and college were a party; I usually ended up blacked out, throwing up, waking up next to a stranger, and mostly clueless about what I had done. I would spend the next three days recovering, then do it all over again.

Once, when I was eighteen, I left a party completely drunk and totaled my car. Fortunately, the friend I was with and I weren't hurt, and the cops never came to the scene. But that still didn't stop my drinking.

When I left for college, I knew that things would not be okay in my family's household. I had taken the burden on my shoulders of keeping my mom and dad's marriage together, and with every phone call home I knew that it was all crumbling. Then my dad got sick with ulcerative colitis, and I had to watch the strongest and most dependable man in my life turn into a skeleton, a shell of himself. This was during the 2008 financial crash, and his law firm was barely staying afloat. Money was scarce. The future was daunting. I didn't know how to deal with it.

I had no tools besides alcohol — lots of it — and this became my coping mechanism.

Then came my love affair with Adderall, an amphetamine that allowed me to study all day, not eat a single bite of food, clean the house, spend two hours getting ready, then party all night. Because I would then drink a liter of vodka with no food, the alcohol poisoning would leave me sick in bed, throwing up for days on end. Then I would recover and do it all again. It was self-abuse, and at some level I knew it, but as I watched my weight plummet and my delusions soar, I just couldn't stop.

My grades were fine, and I was pretending to be a normal, functioning college student. I even pretended to love my body, since I'd been overweight as a younger teen and was thin now. But inside I hated myself. I hated that I needed alcohol to have fun, that I chose my own fun over making my parents' marriage work (as if that was ever my responsibility), and that I was creating so many drunken regrets.

One day I was driving up to Newport Beach from my home in San Diego for a party with some much older "friends." I had the music blasting, Adderall running through my veins, vodka soda in my cupholder, and a cigarette between my lips. My phone rang. It was my brother. He said, "You need to turn around and come home right now. Something is wrong with Dad." I was sick of these calls; I'd had enough of dealing with family drama. So I said, "No. I'm not coming home. I'll be back later tonight." I had to set a boundary. It had been a year of nonstop chaos as my dad's Vietnam War PTSD combined with an entire concoction of Western medicine prescriptions took his mind into severe mania. Something I had never seen in him before. It was a dark force, it was destructive, and it was traumatic for our entire family. One day was him going missing when he decided to go on a solo sailing trip hundreds of miles into the Pacific Ocean without telling anyone, including his entire law office staff and clients. Another day was him totaling his car, getting arrested for a DUI, and being put in a mental institution mandated hold. It was nothing short of horrifying to watch.

I drove back down to San Diego about ten o'clock that night, drinking on the way home and smoking weed. There was a party bus on its way to my house to pick up my roommates and fifty of our friends so we could go clubbing downtown. I called my brother and told him he could meet me at my house for ten minutes before I needed to get ready to go out. At this point, I remember feeling like I didn't have anything left in me to give to the family drama. I wanted to get wasted with my friends as soon as I could to try to forget the endless bad dream I was stuck in.

He and my mom were waiting at my front door when I pulled my car into the driveway. Their faces were grave. I felt a sudden stab of anxiety. My brother walked into my bedroom for privacy, and he didn't waste any time breaking the news: "Dad is dead."

Time slowed down to a halt. It felt like I had slipped between dimensions of reality. I felt an instant, deafening sound pitch in my head. I gathered myself enough to ask, "How?"

"He took his life," he said with big tears in his eyes.

WHAT. THE. FUCK. My dad committed suicide? Anger,

rage, confusion, sadness, despair, and shame flooded me. My entire world collapsed around me. My body turned cold. I don't even remember what I said, but I do remember I was screaming. I was drunk, I was high on amphetamines, and I had just received the most painful news of my life.

My dad was a major source of love, connection, and safety in my life, and I would miss him terribly. For the next year, I went from bad to worse. After three months of suffering an excruciating pain that felt like an ice pick was in my jaw, I was diagnosed with a serious jawbone infection from a previous unhealed wisdom tooth surgery and had to have major recon-structive surgery on my jaw. I went on a three-day drug binge at the Electric Daisy Carnival in Las Vegas and took the party way too far this time — multiple nights with zero to two hours of sleep, saying yes to any substances offered to me from seedy characters. I remember running around that festival feeling soulless, searching to feel something, anything. Drugs and al-cohol were the only way I knew how to cope, but for a sensi-tive girl like me, it only made my anxiety worse. A lot worse. I didn't want to face the pain of my life. I tried not to notice my mom refusing to live after my father was gone. Life just felt so scary. It *was* so scary.

The whole time I was pretending: pretending that I was okay with my dad's death, pretending that I was healthy, pre-tending that I was happy. But I wasn't, and pretending became harder and harder. Finally, one day when I was twenty-one, I realized I was at a crossroads. It dawned on me that no one was coming to save me. I had to save myself. It was like a moment where the dark clouds parted and I could see two distinct paths for my life. Either I could continue down the same road I had been on and end up severely hurt or dead, or I could wake the fuck up and start healing. I saw an alternative path where I could look behind me to see what I was running from and figure out whether I truly had to keep running or I could actually find the courage to face what terrified me.

I chose the latter. It was an unforgettable moment of awakening. Slowly, I began tapping into the worlds of personal development, energy healing, transformational work, trauma clearing, and working through childhood wounds. Everything in me wanted to run from the pain that came up, but I knew I couldn't anymore; running was killing me. I took every course, read every book, and attended every seminar that I could get my hands on. I entered into a heaven-sent relationship in which my partner held me to a standard of no drugs or other sexual partners. There were nights when I felt like my world was shattering open, but I kept going, even when I thought the pain inside me would surely kill me.

My life began to change.

This book is for every woman out there who is at a crossroads in her life and ready for a big change. For every woman who needs a loving hand of support, an objective perspective, and someone to give her a little kick in the booty to remind her who she truly is: a fucking badass warrior gift from God who has every right to take up space on planet Earth and shine her light like the divine, radiant being that she is. Look in the mirror, sister. I'm talking to you!

If you, like so many women, are one of the tenderhearted who has been disillusioned with life, believing that what you want is too big, that your pain is too much, that your dreams are too lofty, that your body is too imperfect to flaunt, that your imagination is too wild, and that your dreams are too unrealistic to bring to fruition, then this book is for you. I ask only that you be open to receiving these truths about yourself: the truth of your own miraculous existence and the truth of your incredible resilience and potential to rebound and return to yourself.

I've been there, beautiful woman. I've come through the fire, and I want to show you how I found myself in the ashes, so you can have your phoenix rise, too.

So who am I *now*?

Today, I'm a woman who has dared to live my truth, beyond what I ever would have believed possible when I started this awakening journey at twenty-one. I have become a woman wild with passion, who recognizes my own tattered heart and loves it anyway. I have become unwilling to accept anything less than total devotion to the pursuit of destiny while I am alive in this human experience, and yet I fall down all the time. I'm a messy, faulty, magnificent masterpiece — just like you are.

I have become a woman who is bold — who expects success, prosperity, and power, like I expect the sun to rise each morning. A woman who is willing to live my life dripping with abundance, luscious with pleasure, and so fucking sparkly that my energy overflows all over the women I guide, teach, and coach, giving them permission to glitter without shame and claim the prosperity that has always been theirs. My love has grown so big that it has transmuted even the darkest pain, and it continues to triumph over darkness. I have stepped out of the darkness and into my light — just like you can.

I am from a generation that was set up to reject the norms, embrace technology, catalyze the mass exodus out of corporate careers and into internet entrepreneurship, reject homophobia, and challenge our elders about race and equality. I am impatient with intolerance and rich with love for all souls, but all this glorious, life-loving, self-loving confidence and prosperity didn't come easily. It was hard won. I would like to start this book out by inviting you into my world — as it is now, but also as it was when I wished I'd had a book like this to read myself.

You see, I understand what it feels like to hurt, to not know why you're stuck, to not be able to see what you're running from, and to lose yourself in pretending it's all okay. I was lost in this maze for years. I was blessed with people who came into my life and gently (or sometimes not so gently) guided me to where I am now. They helped me see that I was the creator of my life experience, that my choices had consequences, and that I could either keep making myself the victim of my circumstances or choose to write a new story.

I would love to be one of those people for you.

The reading journey that you are about to take relates my path to self-discovery and offers a road map for yours. It contains the top breakthroughs that helped me start to understand who I am, why I'm on the planet, and what my greater purpose for being alive is. It also contains my guidance for how you can realize these things, too, not just theoretically but fully and completely, within the depths of your soul.

If you're reading this book, I'm pretty sure I know two things about you: (1) you have a story, and (2) you're beautiful.

Whatever you've gone through (or are still going through) has left you with some level of emotional, mental, spiritual, and/or physical pain, manifesting as energetic weight, that you are ready to be free of. While you've gotten pretty good at holding things together on the surface, you still feel that struggle underneath it all, hampering your efforts to find joy and brilliance.

I hear you. I get it.

You may have a story of trauma and abuse greater than mine, or you may not. You may have a story of addiction similar to mine, or maybe your distractions look or have looked different. Maybe it's people-pleasing, food, sex, shopping, toxic relationships, or simply denial of Self. Wherever you are and wherever you've been, it really doesn't matter. You know you want something different; you know something else is possible; and you're open to learning how to get there, whatever it takes. You are a brave soul to travel this earth at this time in history. You are here on earth because you have a mission to accomplish. No one is here accidentally — not you, not anyone. It is my deep honor to guide you on a journey to uncover that purpose and to feel the depth of the joy, power, and spiritual gifts that you already possess.

If you're still reading, that tells me you're ready. It's time to open up to a life of extraordinary happiness and possibility. It's time to turn on your creatrix superpowers, that part of you that knows how to create your life on command. This life experience gets to be your paradise if you choose it to be. Will you join me in that life? I'm here to help you reach your next-level awakening. Let's begin.

I Am Infinite *Possibility*

As women, we are natural wild feelers. From the moment we start developing as young girls, we are sponges to our environment and the emotions of others around us. Can you remember the intensity and range of your childhood emotions?

Many of us were acutely aware, whether consciously or unconsciously, of our family dynamics. The family (in any form) is where our emotional lives incubate. Whether you had a mostly emotionally functioning home or a blatantly dysfunctional one, you likely experienced strong, keen, painful emotions and at some point had to learn how to shut them down to protect yourself.

Here is the secret at the heart of all human life.

Emotional shutdown is the source of your limitation and pain.

Emotional freedom is the source of your possibility and prosperity.

Emotional Pain, Spiritual Power

Oh, how emotions can hurt us! And oh, how they can induce such euphoria! The feminine range of feeling is not to be underestimated. From the deep shame children so often feel when they think they've disappointed their parents to the glorious glee of those memorable childhood "best days ever"; from the wrenching feeling of having your heart yanked out of your chest by a lover's betrayal to the ecstatic highs of freedom; from the terrifying pull of fear at the thought that someday this will all be over to the euphoria of being totally and completely present in a moment of awe at the beauty of life — for better or for worse, emotions rule us.

We all have emotions, but I believe (with some exceptions) that women feel them in a different, more intense, dare I say deeper way than men. Yes, we are wild, feeling creatures. Let's own that! It's a strength, not a weakness, no matter what some might say. But when we lack awareness about what our emotions are trying to communicate to us, we can become completely controlled by them, unable to choose a rational thought because the emotion is so overpowering. Do you know that feeling? I sure do. And when it happens, what do we do? We run from it, and it chases us down and forces us to do things we wouldn't do in a calmer state of mind. So we fear it. We look away. We bury it.

So many of us have no idea what to do with our strongest emotions, and we don't really know what they mean. But we do know that it seems like they control everything. They can feel inescapable, threatening, embarrassing, and incredibly inconvenient.

Have you ever tried to enjoy a beautiful, sunny day with friends, but you can't stop thinking about what your other friend said to you last night? Your mind is replaying a scenario, causing you to stir with unwanted feelings.

Or have you ever tried to be happy at your friend's wedding, but you can't shake the feeling of grief and sadness that "the one" is not by your side for this special event?

Or have you ever had a lovely, bright start to your Monday and then checked your bank account and felt a crawling dread inch up your spine without warning? Or have you ever woken up and stepped on the scale and suddenly felt the whole day turn into a shame spiral?

Our emotions are a central part of our human experience — and they are so precarious, so easily triggered, so volatile! They're an automatic response caused by chemical reactions in the brain. Most often, we can't choose them. However, what we can do is choose how we respond to them, and that, my beautiful friends, is the secret to emotional mastery.

Emotions are essentially energy in motion. Think of them as swirling energies, not bound by time or space, that live inside of you until you clear them out. They exist in layers — light, transient ones; familiar ones that come and go; and those deep, heavy ones that have been with you for years, that shift seismically every so often, when you least expect it.

But they can all be cleared. The ones that plague you, those you can coax to the surface. To do that, though, requires going into the past to heal. Those deep emotions don't care that they were created when you were five years old, even though now you're twenty-five or thirty-five or forty-five or even a hundred and five. Once they enter you, they become untied from their triggering event, and they settle in and live there until you kick them out. They transcend time and space.

I've spent much of my life feeling confused and distanced

from my emotions, but that's not the way to clear them. The sadness, jealousy, anger, embarrassment, doubt, and insecurity I held inside of me felt like a disease in my body. I hated being hijacked by a feeling and not knowing how to change it, and I couldn't even see how much those stuck emotions were limiting my perceptions and abilities in life. It still happens to me often, and it can be frustrating if it's something I feel I've worked on time and time again. The difference now is that I know there is a gift for me inside of every emotional trigger, a new pathway to accessing more of my power — if I'm willing to feel and heal.

I also couldn't see an important truth: emotions are not a weakness — they are actually a superpower! They limit you only when you refuse to process them. A free emotion is strength. A suppressed emotion can undermine everything about your greatness.

Emotions Are Signals

When was the last time you felt totally hijacked from reality by an unwanted emotion? When did an emotion last make you say or do something you didn't want to say or do? Did you clear it, or is it still in there somewhere, waiting to hijack you again?

When an emotion disrupts us, it's not because we let it out, even if that's how it feels. It's actually because we are fighting it, hanging on to it, grasping at it, or trying to push it down. We are holding on instead of letting it blow through us like the storm that it is, then allowing it to move on.

Emotions are signals. They are what we feel when our brain chemistry is alerting us to something important, whether it's something wonderful or something terrible. They come from a complex alchemy of hormones, like serotonin, dopamine, oxytocin, cortisol, and epinephrine, that are tied to safety and survival and that rise and fall according to our brain's perceptions of reality. They are signs that we should do something, or that we shouldn't do something, or that we should pay attention. They arise within us for good reason.

But what do we do? Instead of listening to the message at the heart of the emotion, we fight it, or we get scared or threatened by it, or we hold on to it like we don't ever want to let it go. Whether it's love or hate, anger or joy, so often we get the signals all wrong.

If you want to grow in this lifetime and tap into the infinite field of magic, prosperity, orgasmic pleasure, and adventure, you must be willing to explore the forces of emotions, as daunting as that may seem. You must be willing to feel them fully, and you must also be willing to let them go.

Neither one is easy.

If you knew how to remove the single greatest obstacle to having it all in your life — the body, the wealth, the relationship, the freedom — wouldn't you choose to do it? What if I mentioned that there is a cost? Would you be willing to pay it? The exchange is that you are going to have to start feeling your feelings, even when you think they might kill you. Then you are going to have to let them go, even if you think you'll die without them.

Feelings are meant to be felt, and then they are meant to dissipate. We aren't supposed to pretend they aren't there, and we aren't supposed to hang on to them like they are the answer to all our problems.

To refuse to feel is to suppress, and that makes emotions get stuck inside. To refuse to let go is to get stuck in a repeating loop, and that makes emotions get stuck inside, too. To feel and release will free you from every heavy emotion and mental torment that keeps you stuck. It will open you to an inner freedom, full of power and pleasure beyond your comprehension.

So how do you do it?

Awareness is the path to healing. In order to access awareness, you must be present with your emotions and allow yourself to feel, even when it's uncomfortable — especially when it's uncomfortable. In our fast-paced lives, it's far too easy to stay distracted from feeling. You're going year after year, running at life, to some invisible finish line. Guess what happens when you get there? Often, a huge letdown when you realize that you're not as happy and fulfilled as you imagined you'd be. Has this ever happened to you? Or have you seen this happen to someone you love? This is your invitation to slow down, to feel, and to commit to your healing. I promise you, it's worth it.

Sacred Cycles of Seven

When I was relearning to feel my emotions, I spent a lot of time doing inner child healing. My inner little girl was carrying a heavy load of fear, sadness, and shame. It was a lot to unpack. (I'm still unpacking it, as I'm committed to my little girl for life.) As I was healing, I was able to clearly see three main development cycles in my upbringing. When I did research, I wasn't surprised to find these development cycles in countless bodies of work.

Using the cycles of seven to track my own healing gave me a helpful framework. Throughout history and across many spiritual sects, we see the number seven in relationship to cycles and healing. These cycles relate to the stages in which our emotions develop, and they run deeply through many facets of our design as humans, through patterns in nature, and even through the way our world and our societies operate. Here are some examples:

- NATURE: The number seven is much more prevalent in nature than most of us realize. There are seven oceans, seven continents, seven vertebrae in most mammals' necks, and seven layers of skin on our bodies. The rainbow has seven colors, and in music, each major scale has seven notes.

- HINDUISM AND THE SEVEN CHAKRAS: In Hinduism seven is considered a sacred number representing the days of the week, the colors in a rainbow, the musical sounds, and more. Also, Hinduism gave rise to the yogic tradition, which recognizes the seven chakras, energy vortexes that run along the spinal column. Each one is connected to various glands and organs, as well as to the life energy of a human being. The full alignment of the seven chakras represents optimal health, both physically and spiritually.

- JUDAISM: This world religion has many connections to the number seven, including the seven candles of the menorah, which is used for worship, and the biblical belief that the earth was created in seven days (counting a day of rest).

- CHRISTIANITY: The seven-day week in Christian tradition represents the time it took God to create the universe and humankind. The number seven is associated with completeness and perfection. Seven has been regarded as having sacred power, as in the seven cardinal virtues, seven deadly sins, and seven sacraments.

- ISLAM: Seven circumambulations are made around the Kaaba. Pilgrims perform seven walks between Al-Safa and Al-Marwah during Hajj and Umrah. It is believed that the number of doors to hell is seven. Almighty (Allah) mentions the number seven in the Qur'an in chapter 2, verse 29: "It is He Who hath created for you all things that are on earth; then He turned to heaven and made them into seven firmaments; and of all things He hath perfect knowledge."

- BUDDHISM: Seven is the number of ascent in the Buddhist tradition. The Buddha is also said to have walked seven steps at his birth.

- ARISTOTLE: A famous quote from the Greek philosopher reads, "Give me a child until he is seven, and I will show you the man," suggesting that the seven-year cycles of development in children have long been observed.

- GREEK MATHEMATICS: Pythagoreans believed the number seven pointed to the union of the spiritual (symbolized by the number three) with the physical (symbolized by four).

- RUDOLF STEINER: An early twentieth-century philosopher and mystic, Steiner conceived a theory of development in three seven-year cycles based on developmental milestones in relation to astrology. Each phase is connected to a different facet of mental and emotional growth and to a specific planetary influence.

- **THE GENE KEYS:** This channeled body of teachings for self-discovery also describes the emotional development of humans in three seven-year cycles, from birth to age twenty-one. In these foundational years, our brains develop, and our emotional landscape is created.
- **NUMEROLOGY:** The number seven is the number of the spirit and the inner world.
- **ECONOMICS:** In previous decades we have seen several major economic downturns hitting in seven-year cycles, including in 1966, 1973, 1980, and 2008.

There is something undeniably true about the universal cycle of seven, and it's been tracked since the beginning of time. You are a beautiful divine creature of the earth, made up of the vast intelligence of the earth, and the cycles of seven apply to you, too.

The entirety of your emotional identity developed in three seven-year stages, forming the core imprinting of who you are. In order to unlock your most empowered, sexy, and free self, you must access the energetic baggage that accumulated at each of these stages and free yourself from the emotions that have been frozen there. You can do it, girl; I believe in you.

Here are the three stages that I mapped in myself, using the template of the seven-year cycle of development:

1. **AGES ZERO TO SEVEN: YOUR POWER.** Your core fear beliefs about personal power, safety, attachment, belonging, and acceptance.
2. **AGES SEVEN TO FOURTEEN: YOUR FEMININITY.** Your core fear beliefs about femininity, womanhood, and emotional expression.

3.   **AGES FOURTEEN TO TWENTY-ONE: YOUR FREEDOM.**
Your core fear beliefs about your place in the world, your creative self-expression, and your self-efficacy.

Let's break this down further, shall we?

1. Ages Zero to Seven: You as Mother

For the first seven years of life, your entire existence centers around trying to make sense of this reality and discover whether you are safe here. Every single fear you feel today can be traced back to this time. The reason we shower young children with fairy and folktales comes down to exactly this: to instill the belief that the world is safe. Do you remember Cinderella? Snow White? Mulan? The idea that good overcomes evil was deeply satisfying to you as a little girl.

You came into this world as a spiritual being, sent from the heavens, with a unique mission, and when you entered the womb and started growing as a fetus, your experience of the world was entirely merged with your mother's experience. Her nervous system was the first vibration of planet Earth that you felt. You didn't know yourself as anything other than her. Her fears, her passions, her sadness, her joy — her emotions — were all yours.

In essence, you *were* her.

In these early years, as you were still one with your mother, you began to develop your identity and interact with the world around you as if you were a sponge. You spent your days drinking up the world and soaking in every single vibration. You were just beginning to discover and develop your physical body and your physiological rhythms. The patterns you developed at this stage make up the core of your identity. This is the period of life when you decided what you believed to be true about yourself. This was the birth of your self-esteem.

More than likely, this is when your first trauma happened. The world was harsh, and you felt it. When this imprinting occurs, it creates a split in our energy, and it stays suspended in time until it's properly integrated. When it is left unintegrated for a lifetime, we develop poor self-esteem, self-confidence, and self-worth.

Freeing your inner little girl from her original pain opens up a vast emotional freedom. You can access your imagination, your creativity, your childlike wonder of the world, your innocence, your playfulness, and your weightlessness.

You get to enter into the eternal moment of the universe — where you can rest in presence, peace, and stillness — because your mind is free from the primal fears of wondering whether it is safe for you to live.

Ages Zero to Seven: Central Questions

- What am I?
- Is it safe for me to exist?
- Is the world safe?
- Will others support me when I need them?

ASK YOURSELF

What do you remember from ages zero to seven? I invite you to get out a journal and to write and reflect on the questions and prompts below.

- Do you know anything about your mother's pregnancy? What do you imagine you were feeling from her while in her belly?
- Who were you as a young child? Have you been told any stories about yourself at that stage? Write about yourself from the perspective of your inner little girl.
- Can you think of a time when you had a strong and memorable emotion as a child between the ages of zero and seven? What was happening? What were you feeling?

When you are finished, spend time in quiet contemplation. Breathe. Know that no matter what was happening when you were a little girl, you are now safe to feel and process.

BONUS EXERCISE: *Visit joliedawn.com/esf to experience a guided journey for accessing memories from ages zero to seven. This will help you to powerfully feel, integrate your emotions, and heal.*

2. Ages Seven to Fourteen: You as Your Own Person

This second cycle is where the core of your emotional development occurs. As puberty happens — hello, hormones, breasts, and body hair — it's the time when you experience your femininity and womanhood. Remember when crushes were so significant? This is also when you learn your primary emotional defense mechanisms, whether you are safe to feel and express emotions or if you need to numb and repress them in order to get by. And, as our brain continues to develop, we begin to get a sense of what is right and wrong in the world.

The emotional patterns you developed were an adaptation so that you could feel safe in the world around you. If you think about it, it's pretty amazing how we learned to adapt to the world. We have complex psychological systems to help us make sense of our reality and protect us from danger. The problem with emotional adaptation is that what used to work when we were ten doesn't necessarily work for us as adult women. Many women have a lifelong relationship with highly fluctuating or very suppressed, numbed emotions. The emotional patterns you established during this time get triggered whenever you feel unsafe in the world. These become the energetic weight that you no longer need as a grown adult.

And when your inner ten-year-old is pissed off and frustrated with authority, it's hard to be the queen of your reality, grounded and clear as an adult woman.

When we begin to heal and integrate the early trauma to our femininity and self-expression in stage 2, we can embrace a life of feeling safe to experience and express our emotions.

The way I think of masculinity and femininity is simple. The masculine energy is the sperm, and the feminine is the egg. The sperm has a directed focus of where to be, a mission to accomplish, a linear, mathematical direction to go in. The egg is the space for all life; she is true receptivity at her core.

In most Western schools, we were taught in a logic-centric, or what I would regard as a more masculine, form of learning. We used intellect instead of imagination. To me, imagination and creativity are more feminine forms of learning. Stage 2 is when many women shut down parts of their femininity and their connection to their heart, opting instead for masculinity and overthinking. Many of us unconsciously emulated men in order to succeed and to be respected and safe.

At stage 2, most girls begin the process of puberty and embrace the female cycle of menstruation. Our bodies develop curves and body hair, and we begin to look more like women than children. During this time of female maturation, we learn some critical beliefs about what it means to be a woman and whether it's safe to be a feminine woman or not. We learn about our sexuality and if we are safe in our bodies. We learn whether our emotional vulnerability is acceptable or not.

Enter the age of anxiety. Most adults who suffer from moderate to severe anxiety have painful memories and emotions from stage 2 layered in their energetic body. When you learn that it's not safe to feel your emotions, you end up living some version of a masculine-dominated, hyperdetermined way of being, shut down partially or fully from feeling. You end up identified with your mind, and we all know that can be a very scary and dangerous neighborhood.

Anxiety disorder tends to affect more women than men. Why is that?

Because we are wild feelers, and if we aren't being true to our natures, we repress emotions that later come back to haunt us.

Because we tend to feel more responsible for other people's happiness than men do and carry a burden of pleasing the people we love.

Because we are taught that intellect is more valuable than emotions, and we likely haven't had many safe places to process the experiences of our lives, especially as wildly hormonal teenagers.

What often happens is that our emotions didn't find a safe place to be expressed, so as adults our mind kicks into overdrive, causing us to spin out, worry, think obsessive thoughts, avoid, endlessly question ourselves, and feel a recurrent insecurity.

Ages Seven to Fourteen: Central Questions

- Who am I?
- Is it safe for me to feel?
- Am I safe being a woman?
- Is the world a kind and just place?

ASK YOURSELF

What do you remember from ages seven to fourteen? I invite you to get out a journal and to write and reflect on the questions and prompts below.

- Who were you during this time? Have you been told any stories? Write about yourself from the perspective of yourself at this age.
- What was your experience of getting your period, or not getting your period? What did puberty bring up for you?
- How did you feel around others, in your life and in school? Did you feel safe to express your emotions, like sadness, fear, anxiety, rejection, or self-doubt? Did you have adults to confide in?
- What did femininity mean to you?

When you are finished, spend time in quiet contemplation. Breathe. Feel that you are now safe.

BONUS EXERCISE: *Visit joliedawn.com/esf to experience a guided journey for accessing memories from ages seven to fourteen. This will help you to powerfully feel, integrate your emotions, and heal.*

3. Ages Fourteen to Twenty-One: You in the World

The final stage of the three cycles is when your core mental development happened. Research shows that the brain completes development at age twenty-one. (That's why the drinking age in the United States is twenty-one. However, I began my love affair with alcohol at fourteen. As an extremely shy girl, it was my ticket to self-expression.) During this time, you learn to use your mind to control your outside world. Often, this is when women learn to override their incredible intuitive superpowers to fit into a masculine world, thus embracing mental intellect over imagination and creativity.

During this phase, young adults begin to question everything — authority, justice, and what is true. This phase is characterized by idealism. In stage 3, you form a new kind of identity — the character of who you are in the world — which will stay with you until you reclaim your true self-expression.

Many of us were in a formal school environment when we were developing our mental intellect. We were determining:

- Am I smart compared to others?
- Do I feel like I'm going to make it in the world?
- Am I confident in who I am, or am I safer following the crowd?

In the modern school environment, we were introduced to lifelong imprints of stress and anxiety. School was daunting, and college and the "real world," which were approaching fast, were built up to be a very big deal. For many people, this was a scary prospect. Without even realizing it, we began to predict whether we were going to be successful in life or not. We were learning whether we could trust ourselves or if authority was always the default to trust.

In the West, we are taught to be obsessed with the intellect instead of using the imagination and creativity. We fear the unpredictability of creativity and value the predictability of linear thinking. Artists unfortunately end up being on the fringes of society. Most of us developed a fear of our success, because society placed the highest value on fitting in (ouch!). If left unchecked, this fear permeates everything we pursue in life.

People often stay frozen in time at this stage of development. A lot of women learned that it was just too stressful to try to do life on their own, and they sought out the support of others. Many married young just for safety instead of following their dreams. I'm not saying that marrying your high-school sweetheart is bad or wrong, but if you did it because life alone felt too hard, then you may not have reached your maximum purpose, thus your maximum happiness.

Ages Fourteen to Twenty-One: Central Questions

- Do I relate to myself as successful, capable, and responsible?
- How much do I trust my ability to create my place in the world?
- Do I feel confident and ready to enter adulthood?
- Are my imagination and creativity safe?

ASK YOURSELF

What do you remember from ages fourteen to twenty-one? Journal on the questions and prompts below.

- When you were in school, did you feel smart or successful?
- How was your self-esteem? Did you feel safe to be an individual? Did you feel like you had self-worth and self-respect?
- Did you stand up for yourself?
- Did you feel safe to enter the "real world"?

When you're finished, spend time in quiet contemplation. Breathe. Feel that you are safe.

 BONUS EXERCISE: *Visit joliedawn.com/esf to experience a guided journey for accessing memories from ages fourteen to twenty-one. This will help you to powerfully feel, integrate your emotions, and heal.*

The three stages of emotional development I outlined above encompass how our psyche developed — the totality of our minds, the unconscious and the conscious. In essence, how we developed in those first twenty-one years set in motion patterns of our thinking and our emotions that will continue to rule our lives until we create new neural pathways in our brains.

Accessing Awareness to Reclaim Your Power

I believe the master teachers have been saying the same thing for thousands of years. The Buddha said, "Look inward." Plato and Socrates said, "Know thyself." We know we need to look to ourselves to find our magic, our purpose, the kingdom of heaven that somehow lives inside us. Yet we don't do it. Why not?

The answer to that complicated question begins in child-hood.

Imagine the five-year-old version of you. The cute little girl that you used to be, all dressed up for your first day of kindergarten. Maybe you were nervous, or excited, or terrified, and when you walked into that classroom, maybe it was everything you hoped for, or everything you feared. But I can make a pretty good guess about one thing: on that first day, you were put into a box. You were told where to sit, how to behave, what you were supposed to learn, and how you were supposed to learn it. You didn't get to create the box. It was created for you.

For the next thirteen years of your life, until you graduated from high school, you had to stay mostly within the confines of that box — at least, you did if you wanted to do well in school, make your teachers and parents proud of you, and have a chance at the boxed version of success. If you went to college, your box may have gotten a bit bigger, but it was still a box. There were rules, and they applied to everyone.

It didn't matter who you were. Your uniqueness, your individuality, was *not* nurtured. You couldn't really be fully yourself. How could you be as big and bright and beautiful as you truly were when you were inside a box? Chances are, your greatest concern was just surviving and fitting in and not making too much of a fuss — but in following those box rules, the very essence of you was at great risk of getting buried. No wonder so many of us don't know, or forgot, how brilliant we really are!

There is no room for strong emotions inside of a box. That is why we bury them. And that is why they haunt us.

Good news, sister. Together, we're on the journey to unearth that essence — the you that you always were and are ready to be again.

In order to find out your unique brilliance — what your thing is to do in the world and why it's specifically *yours* to do — you have to remember *who you really are*. It's already inside of you. It lives in your soul. You just have to allow it to show itself. And in order to do that, you need to look at where you've been stopped in your complete expression, in fully creating and becoming whatever you want to be.

Kids are often told they can be anything that they want to be, but as adults, this doesn't usually feel true at all. Somewhere along the way, as we grew and matured inside the box, we accepted that reality and began to live it on autopilot. The direction was set, so you coasted, like a self-driving car. But do you know what a self-driving car really is? A robot.

Robots do not experience happiness, joy, and personal fulfillment, and you won't find those feelings by living on autopilot. *Your* happiness, *your* joy, *your* self-expression exist only when you're able to create your life and fully feel your emotions *outside the box*. This is the only way to discover who you are beyond who you have been told and expected to be.

This may surprise you, but you have the power to make a conscious choice about *every single piece of your life*. You may have been handed a long list of "supposed tos" and "right things to do" and qualifications for being a "good girl," but just because someone hands you instructions doesn't mean you have to follow them.

It's not your fault the world that you grew up in was more concerned with how you should fit in and be the same as everyone else than with how you were unique. It's not your fault that nobody really, deeply nurtured your creativity and explained to you how essential it was (as opposed to being a "waste of time" or "impractical"). You were probably never offered the Blasting into Your Creative Potential 101 class.

Well, guess what? As of this moment, I give you full permission to blast open, kick free of the box, color outside of the lines, and live fully and completely beyond what you think is possible, so you can find your way right into the center of your unique and magnificent creative genius. This is how and where you access the brilliance of you. Now more than ever, the world needs you to show up and to share your gift!

I give you permission to dream. I give you permission to step outside of what you were told that the limitations of this reality were. Limitations like "It's hard to make money" or "I have to sacrifice to survive" or "I have to do a job in order to get experience before I can do my thing in the world." These limitations no longer have power over you. It's time to choose possibility.

How will you know when you have entered the world of possibility? You will see yourself as the powerful creator that you truly are, moving wildly in the direction of your dreams, taking a one-way ticket to a far-off country, never putting separation between you and the things you want. You will feel you're worthy enough to have everything that you want in this lifetime.

Don't know what that is yet? Then dream it. You have permission right now to dream. What would your life be like if there was no box? Who would you be if you weren't trying to be what other people told you to be? Let your mind go wild and free with imagining your ideal life, living as the real you, having everything you need and want.

This is the beginning. To dream something is to put it into your conscious mind and see it as a potential reality. The purpose of your life, your true fulfillment and unique brilliance, comes from when you say, "This is what I want, and this is how I want to feel." You command your experience, and limits dissolve. Possibility becomes more like probability.

I can personally speak to this. Before I was in alignment with my true Self, everything seemed difficult. It felt so hard to build my self-confidence, so hard to make ends meet, so hard to trust myself as a responsible adult who could take care of myself and future fully. Now that I am doing what truly turns me on in life (which is to have this very conversation with you and open up space for women to conceptualize and then step into their creative potential and into their power, along with running my high-earning coaching company), things flow much more easily for me. I trust myself. I am setting up my future in a big, real way. It's a good feeling.

I want you to have this easy flow, too. I want you to have a life that *totally turns you on.*

Ease versus Easy

Before we go any further, I want to point out something: there is a difference between ease and easy. Having ease in your life means you respond to life's hurdles with grace, and you are able to pull yourself back to a positive space when something shitty comes at you. You are constantly cultivating an essence of ease, of flow, of acceptance for what is.

This does not mean that life will always be easy. Sometimes you have to take big, hard actions, like cutting off a toxic relationship, apologizing for acting without integrity, or dealing with a loss. You can't always make things easy, but you can always access ease if you choose.

What I really want you to take from this chapter is a new level of awareness of what is truly possible in your life — to understand that a set of beliefs has been passed on to you that keep you in a space of limitation until you realize what they are and stop conforming to them. Instead of shaping yourself into someone else's view of you, it's time to start living in your own shape, feeling your own feelings, and to quit apologizing for being who you are. It's time to start creating dreams that scare the shit out of you because they are so unbelievably big, beautiful, and representative of a life you may never have thought you could really have. Sister, this world is your playground. It's time to play. Your life is a blank canvas, and you're the only one holding the paintbrush. So what will you paint?

ASK YOURSELF

Let's try something right now. This in an invitation to deep contemplation and/or journaling. Stop for a quiet moment. Take a few deep breaths. Focus inward, to that place where your spirit lives, the place in which you originated, beyond the physical, beyond the constraints of the 3D world. Focus on the spiritual essence of you.

Now, get curious. Contemplate these questions if you're feeling eager to tap your inner wisdom.

- Why did I come here? Why me? Why now? Why again?
- What am I here to do? What am I here to experience? What am I here to be of service to?
- Who are my key players in this game? Is there a way to win at this game? If so, how? Is there a way to lose at this game? If so, how?
- How can I be the truest version of myself? How can I heal in order to ascend? Where do I find my power?

- What does it look like to live as a woman who is empowered, sexy, and free?

You don't have to answer a single one of these questions yet. Just ask them. Open up the book of questions within and let them rise up and become manifest in your consciousness. This is how you begin the healing.

Sister, everything that you've been through made you the beautiful, strong, wise woman that you are today. You are a gift of the universe, highly favored, loved, and cherished more than your mind could ever comprehend.

If you're feeling tender right now as you reflect on your childhood development, invite in more love. Love that little girl with all you've got. You are a masterpiece of God's creation, and nothing you went through was in vain. Can you trust that?

In the next chapter, I will let you in on my biggest secret to being a kick-ass, intentional creator in my life. You will move past resistance more quickly than you thought possible, find new depths of self-understanding, and create miracles with ease. Yes! Let's do it!

CHAPTER TWO

I Am the Creatrix of My Life

*I*n this chapter, you are going to get my hands-down favorite tool for creating a sexy life. "What is it?" you ask? Journaling.

Now, before you say, "I already do that," or "I don't like journaling," let me explain how I discovered this powerful writing ritual for myself and how I use it differently than you might think.

In 2013, my life was all wrapped up in a pretty bow. I was engaged to be married to an amazing, successful man, a prolific entrepreneur. He was such a catalyst for me. This is the relationship I called "heaven-sent" in the introduction of this book. When my life was a total mess, at that time in my early twenties, he turned my life around. We talked about being together forever and how we would raise our kids. He was a well-known leader in the community; we were a public couple. I was rising in my transformational coaching career in San Diego, hosting large women's empowerment events as well as intimate women's circles, and everybody looked up to us as the Sweetheart Couple.

I won't ever forget the day I came home from a three-day women's retreat weekend, happy and fulfilled and ready to connect with my fiancé, and he looked me in the eyes and said, "I want to transition out of this relationship." We had never once spoken about breaking up.

As you can probably imagine, I was caught completely off guard. First I was stunned, and after the shock wore off I was terrified. I couldn't imagine or believe that I would be able to take care of myself fully, at the level that I had become accustomed to. After losing my father to suicide, I had immediately jumped into a relationship with this man, who took on the dominant masculine role in my life. That had been a pretty effective way to temporarily ward off all the trauma of my father's death. But with my partner gone, I was going to have to face it all — the whole series of fears that I had unconsciously been putting off fully feeling and honoring.

A few days after this life-changing news, I went to Mexico with a group of girlfriends. I spent some time by myself, looking out over the Pacific Ocean and dropping deeply into the moment. Then, for no conscious reason, I pulled out my journal and starting writing.

That simple act changed me. When it was just me and my journal, the fear and anxiety faded, and I felt a sense of calm and direction come over me. I knew that I was going to be okay. And more than just okay — I was going to thrive. I committed myself to a thirty-day writing practice, and I have been doing this particular method of ritual writing every day (often multiple times per day) since.

Let me tell you, journaling has been a total game changer

for me. It has been the single most important spiritual ritual in my life. It allows me to process emotions, talk to my higher Self and God, deal with triggers, recount my dreams, express gratitude, celebrate myself, build my inner confidante, and deepen my self-awareness. When I look back on my previous entries, I see how much I've grown, how my manifestation superpowers work in action, how the universe has blessed me with so many answered prayers, and how I have continually inspired myself.

Reflecting on your writing, and rereading what you've written, is an essential part of this practice, just as important as writing newly. This allows for an unparalleled way of digesting life, a sense of forward motion, and a chance to slow down and process fully. I don't have another spiritual ritual that fulfills me quite like this practice does. There aren't even words for how grateful I am for my years of devotion to this process and what it's brought to my life. I give it credit for so much of my success and ability to feel sustained inner peace. It has taken me from extreme fear and incessant, unconscious negative self-talk to building myself up as a daily practice through my writing and running a highly profitable coaching empire, impacting thousands of women each year.

Have you ever done any journaling of your own? Most people have tried it at least once. And many of those people find it boring, repetitive, and a waste of time. I can totally relate to that. Based on what I initially thought I was *supposed* to be writing in my journal — recounting my daily experiences, for example — I felt the same way.

But journaling is so much more than a glorified teenager's diary, as I'm about to show you.

The type of journaling I'm talking about connects you deeply to your inner guidance and your inner voice. It silences the noise around you and gives you a way to channel your unique essence and brilliance, shuttling what lives in your subconscious into your conscious mind. If you give this type of journaling a chance, you'll be very surprised at the innate beauty and strength you find within yourself.

In all my coaching programs, taking up a journaling practice is a requisite. There is nothing quite like it to help you start uncovering the real you. It takes a minimum of three weeks to develop a habit, so I invite you to buy yourself a special journal that you love and take up the practice for the next twenty-one days.

My Top Ten Journaling Practices

Need more convincing? Here are the top ten ways to journal that I recommend you try. Sometimes I do one of these a day, sometimes more than one. Sometimes I do one type of entry several days running, and other times I switch them up. You can use them in any way and in any order that feels right to you.

I'm also including examples of each entry type. Since my purpose here is to share my heart with you, these examples are lifted straight from my own journal. You are the first to ever read them. I hope they inspire you!

1. Express Gratitude

When you express what you're grateful for and what you appreciate, your entire vibration expands and heightens, allowing you to attract more things worth your gratitude. It is so easy to forget the magic all around us. Your journal gives you a space to pause and look at your life in awe, with appreciation and acceptance. It gives you a chance to thank your body and your heart. It gives you an opportunity to celebrate what you have accomplished and recognize all that you have (as opposed to focusing on everything you don't have and still want).

I challenge you to write down ten things that you're grateful for every single day, then let these things live in your mind after you've closed your journal. Tell your friends what you're grateful for and ask them what they are grateful for. Start conversations about gratitude. Ironically, appreciating what you already have is part of the process of attracting more of what you want. This is especially useful in times when you feel like you've lost something or don't have enough of something, like money or other resources.

From My Journal:

Today I am waking up and feeling so appreciative to be alive. Thank you, spirit, for all the blessings in my life. I am experiencing prosperity and growth like never before. I am so happy to be here.

Jolie, thank you for all that you've been doing lately to love me. All of the healthy food choices, allowing yourself to receive love from others, and all of the travel adventures. I am full, I am content, I am alive.

I am grateful for my health, my money, my comfort, fresh food, the sunlight, the ocean, my clothes, my laptop, my access to clean water, my knowledge, my heartbeat.

Hello, miracles! I just had my biggest launch to date! YESSSS. Just as I had visualized. Damn, I am magic. Thank you, universe, I am humbly grateful.

2. Process Your Emotions

No one can ever know exactly how you feel except you, and even you might not know exactly how you feel until you start writing about it. Journaling can help you to process and understand what you are feeling. Honor this sacred understanding of yourself. If you feel like crap today, then say it! If you're angry, upset, scared, or confused, then this is your space to let it all out. Write more deeply into it if you aren't sure where those feelings are coming from. Acknowledge what's real for you right now. Maybe you're happy and you want to celebrate. Maybe you want to rant. This is your sacred space, and you may be surprised what you learn about your feelings when you begin writing freely.

From My Journal:

I am bothered today. I feel like a failure. I feel like I'm letting people down. I should be doing more. I should have slept more. I should be creating more. I am fucking annoyed. I'll never be where I want to be if I keep wasting time like this. I miss my house, my room, my safety, my community. Traveling full-time is taking a toll on me. I am emotional. I am scared. I feel guilty as I write this. It's so hard for me to acknowledge any negativity. I feel depleted, out of balance, and off-center. What do I need right now? How can I love myself right now?

✳

This week has been funky. I feel like I've been living in someone else's body. What happened to my magic? I need to surround myself with people who see me. I felt very dismissed by some friends tonight. I don't feel seen or understood. That's okay. I love myself enough to honor my truth and to surround myself with positive, high-vibrational people.

✳

Today I am experiencing sadness. Mourning for an old life. I am here now as I look at the ocean. I am here. This is perfect.

3. Write a Love Letter from Your Higher Self

Your higher Self is the pristine version of you — no ego, no judgments, only divine love. Take a moment to visualize this version of you. Fall in love with her. Know that you already are her. What guidance would she give you? How would she encourage you? What would she say in a love letter to you? You have all the answers within. Trust yourself enough to connect with them.

From My Journal:

Jolie, you are so loved. Enjoy this period of life. Enjoy the journey. Soon you will be busy, so expanded with success. Just be here now and enjoy. Surround yourself with people who honor you and see you. Ask for what you need. Whether you're speaking on stage or brushing your teeth, every moment of life is equally important. I've got you. I love you. You are safe.

❄

Jolie, I am madly, deeply in love with you. A love like I've never felt before. So deep and so eternal, so rich. You are my best friend, my greatest supporter, my lover. I see your beauty; I see your radiance. I am so blessed to see you in this light. Thinking that I get to spend the rest of my life with you lights my entire body up with joy. I love this new relationship with myself. When I am this deeply in love with myself, nothing can stop me.

❄

Breathe... inhale... exhale... acknowledge yourself. There is nothing you need to do, nothing you need to say, nowhere you need to go. You just get to BE.

❄

Jolie, you are not of this world. You came here to experience yourself as human, in physical form. To live a life of remembrance of who you truly are. Breathe in this moment, follow your intuition, be the fullest expression of yourself, be the fullest expression of pure love. Remember, you are the creator of your life. Yes, I am the creator of my life. I am the master of my experience.

4. Send a Message to a Specific Part of Yourself or Your Experience

Cultivate relationships with all things in your life. Talk to inanimate objects as if they have their own consciousness. In my journal, I talk to money, the earth, my business, my body. Seduce money, praise your body, and reclaim your essence. If it feels silly talking to something that isn't a person, good! No one said journals had to be serious all the time. If you want, you can even have the object you're writing to write back to you!

From My Journal:

Dear Money,
I am so excited to expand my relationship with you. I have a fear that you won't forgive me, but I know that's false. All fear is false. I desire to learn more about you and me; I seek to cultivate a loving, mutually beneficial relationship.
    Love,
    Jolie

Dearest Jolie,
This is money talking. Why are you scared of me? I want to play with you. You treat me so well, and we

have so much fun together. Allow me to show up for you. Receive me! I desire to grow with you, and I am so happy that you are ready.

Love,

Money

Dear next event I'm producing,

What contribution do you want to be? Who would you like to have at this event? How would you like me to promote this event? I honor this event as a separate entity. This event is not me. This is far greater than me. I am listening. I am surrendering.

Love,

Jolie

5. Take a Journey through the Present Moment

Drop deeply into the moment and write about what you experience. Witness what is all around you. What do you see? What do you feel? What do your other senses take in? What would you have missed if you hadn't stopped to take in the moment? What thoughts and feelings come up in this state of presence?

From My Journal:

As I stare at the ocean, I see that nature is my greatest teacher. Nature is the greatest reflection of myself. I am reading *The Seven Spiritual Laws of Success* by Deepak Chopra, and these words hit me so profoundly: "I know my desires are inseparably connected to nature. My desires are not my own but rather an evolutionary impulse. Why would I ever doubt them or make them wrong?" That inspires me to think about the natural nature of my own desires.

Like nature, I desire to share my beauty.

Like birds, I desire to be heard.

Like the sun, I desire to shine brightly.

Like the moon, I desire to be in control of the tide of my life.

Like a dolphin, I desire big freedom.

Like grass, I desire to grow abundantly.

Like the seasons, I desire to change with flexibility.

Like water, I desire to be essential to life.

Like a river, I desire to flow with grace.

Like the rain, I desire purity.

Like life cells, I desire to multiply exponentially.

Any remaining guilt for my desires to create and be abundant, I now release. This guilt does not belong to me.

6. Write a Wish List for the Universe

This is your space to place your orders to the universe, just as you would at a restaurant. Would you like something that is currently not in your space? Ask for it, then watch it show up! Remove any guilt that may be attached to you and open yourself up to receiving. Living guilt free is a choice. Receiving is a choice. (We'll talk a lot more about this in chapter 12, "I Am a Manifesting Queen," so stay tuned if you're not sure about this one yet.)

From My Journal:

> Universe, I need a little help here. I need guidance on where I am meant to go next. This lifestyle of traveling full-time is so scary at times. Please show me the next step. Whom am I meant to meet? Where am I meant to go? I request your support to show me the path to my greatest joy, success, growth, and healing.

7. Reflect on Life Lessons

As you go through life, cultivate an awareness of what's unfolding. What makes you sad? What are you not okay with being a witness to? What have you learned in the past that you find applicable now?

From My Journal:

> Today I went to a house party in Pacific Beach. I saw a woman not owning her value. She lost herself. I know her, because I used to be her.
> Damn. SO many of my peers are sleepwalking through life. They have forgotten who they truly are. They are tired, weak, bored, frustrated, lost, and chasing something. They are confused. Life is just passing them by. I feel the pain of this. Assisting the awakening of the

human species is my work to do. I feel the call. God, show me, use me, guide me.

8. Recount Your Dreams

Your journal is a great place to recount your dreams and note how they made you feel. How you felt in a dream is actually more important than what happened in it. You will often find the dream emotions connect to something you are currently feeling in waking life. This can be a great tool for emotional processing, problem solving, facing fears, and gaining a better understanding of current dilemmas or situations.

From My Journal:

My dream last night: I keep having a recurring dream of my deepest fear — that no one really loves me and has my back. In my dream, I was at a party and fell into a thornbush. My back was covered in thorns. When I asked for help to remove them, everyone was too busy. My dad was there, two of my exes were there, and they were all too busy to help me. The thorns represent betrayal.

How I felt in my dream: I've been really struggling with FOMO lately (Fear of Missing Out). When I saw many of my friends at my ex's birthday party, I got really sad. My wounds are deep that people whom I love and need the most will leave me and will not have my back when I need them most. I am feeling sad, scared, and anxious.

How I can love myself today: Today I need to remind myself of who I am and all the love I have in my life. I need to be extra gentle and slow. I need to remember all that I am:

energetic	responsible
passionate	fulfilled
purposeful	taken care of
successful	supported
accomplished	blessed
able to travel	able to enjoy
able to pay rent	making money
able to pay bills	serving others
vibrant	free
healthy	getting results
confident	in community
wise	safe
experienced	secure
in action	appreciated
loved	in flow

9. Make Personal Declarations

As humans, we love to make things real with declarations. Knowing that you can recreate who you are at any given time, whom do you want to be today? Declare it. Claim it. Own it.

From My Journal:

I am power. I am awareness. I am money. I am an infinite being. I am consciousness. I am magic. I am a gift.

I am ready for the fruits of this experience. I have remembered. I am remembrance.

Right now, I declare a new energy of living. I choose to open to new depths of receiving, to invite the experience of massive, inspired action, and to be someone I haven't been in the past. I realize that I have been living in the collective illusion.

When did we start making things so significant? When did money become such a big judge of who we are? When did we start making relationships, breakups, and divorce so significant?

What else is possible?! How easily can we evolve as a species?

I am here. I am grateful. This is it, and it's perfect.

I love myself so much. This new season is a remembrance of my divine feminine power. I love her. I love me. I honor myself. I choose to date myself, take impeccable care of myself, to tune in to my needs before anyone else's. Jolie, you are so fucking awesome. Your life is about to blow you away. Keep asking, "How does it get better?" and you will be shown. Just look at all the magic around you. You are creating this. You hold the magic wand.

10. *Discover Your Own Truth*

Add any other fun and unique content that you like. It's your journal, your expression, and you can fill it up with anything that is meaningful to you. I've seen clients write poems, compose love notes, make food diaries, and use other creative journaling practices.

Feel free to make anything up! Have fun with your journaling and make it your own. This is your space to be creative. Just allow it to flow.

Even if you've never written before or have tried journaling in the past and gave up on the process, I invite you to start here with a clean slate. The promise of this book is that you will have access to discovering the real you and tools to create a life that you love. Accepting my invitations will only speed up the process and leave you with a deeper sense of joy, pleasure, and peace.

Chances are that you experience resistance right now in some area of your life. You may not be able to identify exactly the root cause of it. In the next chapter, we will uncover the areas where potentially you feel stuck, disempowered, and heavy. This will likely open up lots of writing material.

Sister, you possess the power to be a great self-healer. You are more capable than you give yourself credit for, and your higher Self is ready to shower you with wisdom whenever you tap into the source. You are the greatest source of your own healing superpowers. You are the deepest source of love for yourself. You have it all now, you've always had it all, and you will always have it all. Give yourself the gift of going within.

CHAPTER THREE

I Am the Source of

My Power

Tell me if this sounds familiar. You're going about your life. You're having a pretty good day. You're feeling generally positive.

Then, *boom*.

Someone calls, someone says something, something happens, and suddenly you feel annoyed, scared, worried, angry, irritated, terrified, drained of all self-confidence...or just all-over icky.

Maybe you find out your ex just got engaged. Or you look at your almost-overdrawn bank account. Maybe it's just one small comment that someone says to you, like, "Have you found a job yet?" And for the next hour (or day or week) you feel heavy and distracted.

Congratulations. You've just been triggered.

What is this? And why does it happen?

Triggers can be sneaky little devils. You rarely see them coming until they steal the happiness of the moment from you.

In a flash, they convince you that something is wrong (often wrong with *you*), that you need to drop everything else and focus on that one thing, and that the world will end if you don't. Worst of all, they hijack our attention and feel grim, frustrating, and doomful. They rob you of your joy and hold your choices hostage — or at least that's how it feels.

Don't fret, dear one. As humans, we *all* have them.

As an example, one of the most common triggers for adults is money, and the trigger usually originates in childhood. This is certainly the case for me — many of my triggers have to do with money, and it's clear to see how this can be traced right back to my childhood.

When I was growing up, it was always feast or famine in my house. We either had lots of money and I could have whatever I wanted (including a brand-new car on my sixteenth birthday), or we literally had no money, not even enough to buy my school pictures or food. One week we bought a family sailboat, another week my mom's car was repossessed. The stark contrast left me completely confused, with a deep distrust in money.

Both of my parents were challenged money managers, having the attitude that money wasn't important...until there wasn't any left. Then it suddenly became the most important thing in the world. The result was that I grew up with a lot of fear around money. I worried whether we would have enough, if I would have the cool things other kids had (because sometimes I did and sometimes I didn't), and when my parents would have yet another big blowout argument about money.

I'll talk more about parental triggers in the next section, but for now I will say that this fear around money stayed with me into adulthood and was repeatedly activated during my roller-coaster work as an entrepreneur. When you have serious money triggers, there is nothing scarier than not knowing for sure when the next deposit is coming in.

Even though I've worked hard on these and many other common triggers, they are still with me and probably always will be. Triggers don't always disappear (many will!) but they can become much more manageable, so that you feel like you are in control versus them controlling you. Just recently, on Instagram, I saw my closest friends at my ex's birthday party. I felt left out and betrayed that my friends hadn't given me a heads-up. All my mean-girl sisterhood wounds were reactivated. I was tormented in my dreams.

When I saw the Instagram photos, I went into a full-blown trigger mode. I felt nauseous and anxious. I had to take the rest of the day off because I couldn't concentrate, *even though I was in Tulum, surrounded by friends who love the shit out of me, having the actual time of my life.* I just couldn't see it.

The photos brought up all the betrayal fears from the past that I have not fully dealt with. Just like that, I was toast.

Can you think of the last time you felt triggered? What triggers keep coming up for you? At the end of this chapter, we'll talk about ways to begin to understand and control these triggers so they stop controlling you. It's a "play them or be played by them" kind of game.

Your triggers may stay with you for life, but in some ways, you can be grateful for that. Triggers aren't "bad." They actually serve a very particular purpose. Think of them as clues on a treasure map. These little gold nuggets lead you to the issues from your past that still need healing. Follow the triggers, and you'll find the treasure. Believe me, you want to find these treasures, even though they can be very painful. Your freedom depends on your willingness to feel and heal.

For example, if you grew up in an alcoholic home, the smell of alcohol might trigger a negative response in your body. If your first boyfriend was a total player and stood you up at the movies, you may be triggered when someone asks you on a date to the movies. Or maybe when you check your bank account, you are overwhelmed with a fear of scarcity because, like me, you grew up scared that you might not have enough to survive.

This knowledge is your treasure, and once you find it, you can use it to achieve true sovereignty in your emotional experience of life.

We humans are very smart beings. We are constantly learning from the past to prevent making the same mistakes in the future. Triggers are part of this learning mechanism; if you do not deal with them, they will keep coming up to remind you of what you still need to learn. The people and locations and scenarios will be different, but the feelings will be the same. This is a law of the universe.

You have seen this play out with other people. It's your girlfriend who dates the same fuck boys over and over, no matter how clearly you hold up the mirror for her. Or that one friend who always has chaos around her, losing her wallet on a weekly basis, realizing she doesn't have her ID when you're in line at the club, constantly attracting some sort of desperate frenzy.

This is the universe knocking and saying, "Hello! You didn't learn the first time, so I'm sending you different people, events, and situations so you can learn the lesson now! And if you don't get it this time, then we'll keep playing this game till you do."

The Original Trigger Source: Family

There's a saying that goes something like, "If you want to test how far you've come on your personal development journey, go visit your family for a week." No one triggers you quite like your family can. Whether it's your mom, dad, brother, sister, cousin, or all of them, your family is usually all tied up with the formation of most of your triggers. That's because these people represent your closest soul contracts and your closest mirrors. I believe that before we take bodies on planet Earth, we carefully choose who will be the key players in our game — the main actors in our screenplay. These are the people who influence the journey, bring up the issues that need to be resolved, and show us who we are, sometimes in uncomfortable ways. Our souls have contracts with them that need to be fulfilled; that's part of what we are here in this life for.

Parents in particular carry our first and most significant soul contracts. They're also sometimes our most painfully incomplete relationships. Often, before we can progress in every other area of our lives, we have to complete and clean up any junk we have around our parents.

"But Jolie," you might be thinking, "I don't have any issues with my parents! I had a great childhood."

Maybe that's true, if an oversimplification. No childhood is 100 percent bad or 100 percent good. If yours was even 75 percent good, then you are pretty damn blessed, and I honor your wholeness around this topic!

Even so, I'd like to invite you to look again, not because I don't believe you, and not because I want you to manufacture parental issues out of thin air, but because I know that our parents can sometimes be our biggest blind spots. It's easy to overlook how they (usually inadvertently) have shaped our psyches and spawned our triggers.

Here's an example. In my early twenties, when I was on my deep awakening journey, I went to study with an enlightened master from India. I was incredibly conflicted around doing the work with her — I'd grown up Christian, so the very idea of an enlightened master seemed weird and blasphemous to me. I wanted healing from her, but I didn't really want to interact with her or believe in her magic powers. When I got there and found out that the focus of the workshop was to heal our mother-father wounds, I tuned out. I thought that had nothing to do with what I needed.

See, at that point in my life, I thought my childhood was fine. I grew up in the suburbs of San Diego, in a big house on two acres of land with orchards full of fruit trees. I had so much room to play! Seemingly every opportunity was given to me. When I was a kid, I remember starting a fruit stand, then a neighborhood salon. (I was a true entrepreneur hustler from the start.) I lived a very free childhood, and because my parents were in their forties when they had me, with a laid-back attitude, they allowed me to be my own person. This is why I thought that nothing was wrong with my childhood. I didn't know why I was even at the workshop.

Then the moment came for me to face the master and receive her guidance, one on one. I was nervous but also dismissive, until she looked into my face and said very clearly, "Do not have a baby with him."

I felt like a puppet whose strings had just snapped. Aside from her knowing something about me that only I knew — that I really wanted to get pregnant with my boyfriend's baby at that point in my life — she put her finger on a huge parental issue I didn't even know I had. I missed my late dad so much and had so much incomplete healing around him that I wanted to make my boyfriend a daddy and turn *him* into the father figure in my life. I was ignoring the fact that "daddy" was not the right role for him at all. It was not right for me and also not the role he had chosen for himself.

And that was just the beginning. As we spoke more, she pointed out several additional issues that stemmed back to my parents and childhood. I began to realize that in many ways, I was still a hurt little girl living in an adult body. My parents were a blind spot I hadn't wanted to look at. It's not that I went from loving them to thinking they were horrible people. I still loved and appreciated them deeply. But I also saw them more clearly, for who they were: fallible humans who did their best but who nevertheless created some deeply rooted issues in me.

Thus began a journey of exploration back into my past to discover how my childhood influenced my adulthood. A few things stood out to me.

Unfortunately, my parents fought a lot, which is far too common in many families. I remember so clearly the day before my first day of fifth grade. My parents got into a massive fight, and when I went to school I was not able to focus on anything because I was so worried about whether everything was going to be okay at home. Home, for the most part, felt more tumultuous than sanctuary-like.

I was also spiritually confused. Both of my parents were Christians, so we went to church on Sunday morning all buttoned up, but then our family would take vacations in Las Vegas, where my parents would gamble and drink. This seemed inconsistent to me, and I didn't understand it, but I copied it. I sought out spirituality, but I also sought out "sin." I took on the notion that I should obey God on Sunday morning but at night I could be a total rebel. As you can see, I had a lot of healing to do around my relationship with God. (I'll share more on this later.)

Each of my parents did wonderful things for me. My mom taught me to be ultra creative, a free thinker, and a leader. But she also put a strong emphasis on physical beauty and staying young looking. She was judgmental of others and was infatuated with looking her best, which, looking back, seems to me to be rooted in deep insecurity and a need to judge other people in order to feel good about herself. I took this on, as we often take on the beliefs of our parents. I spent much of my life judging other people on their looks — and especially judging myself. Was I pretty enough? Thin enough? Dressed well enough? I rarely felt like it. I had a lot of body insecurity, and I never felt good enough or desirable.

Likewise, my dad taught me all about being empowered, self-sufficient, and intelligent. He always knew how to get the most out of life, to be in a positive mood, and to enjoy every day. I learned this happiness from him. But my dad also had a history of being taken advantage of, and he had a bottomless hole in his bank account. He did not know how to be responsible with money; he would make a lot of money, but he always spent a lot, too, so we never knew whether or not we'd have enough. I took this on as well, learning not to trust myself with managing money and often getting taken advantage of, just like he was.

Their fighting and general instability also put me in a position of feeling like I had to be the responsible one, even though that never should have been my job. So I developed the tendency to take on the role of the caretaker, with a lot of personal boundary issues.

It's incredibly common to live the same patterns our parents lived. This is why abuse, addiction, and alcoholism get passed down from generation to generation — until somebody stops the cycle. This is why, if one of your parents commits suicide, you're seven times more likely to commit suicide yourself. They say women tend to marry their fathers, and it's true that we tend to look for partners who echo the qualities of our parents. I am the perfect example: the issues my parents had with appearance, responsibility, money, and discernment all showed up in my life and became the source of my most significant triggers.

For you the source may be other things. Maybe your dad was a firecracker who had a lot of anger, and you find yourself unable to control your temper. Or maybe your mom was a huge perfectionist, and you find yourself being nitpicky and perfectionist yourself. Maybe one or both of your parents were addicts, and you struggle with substance abuse. Maybe one of them was a workaholic or never found a true passion or direction in life. Maybe one of them left, and you struggle with abandonment or commitment issues. Or they hovered over you all the time, controlling everything, and you never learned how to manage your own life, or you are constantly trying to control others. Maybe they had no ambition or too much ambition. Maybe they were uncomfortable with physical affection. There are as many issues as there are people.

But therein lies the real truth: they aren't your issues. Not really. They are the traits and patterns of your parents, and you only mimic them. The responsibility of being a caretaker and the obsession with physical beauty from my mom, the money fears and tendency to get taken advantage of from my dad — none of those traits actually belonged to me. I didn't agree to take them on or make a soul contract with them.

The good news is that since these things are not your issues, you can free yourself from holding them as your burden.

I know, it can feel impossible to free yourself. Why do we hold on to patterns, beliefs, judgments, and opinions that aren't really ours? Partially because, consciously or not, on some level we all want to *be* our parents. On another level, we want to be whatever they wanted us to be. So we allow ourselves to live the lives that they handed to us — whether they meant to hand us those exact lives or not. My mom didn't intend to hand me insecurity. My dad didn't try to hand me fear around money. But because I allowed myself to take them on, those issues showed up in my life.

Your family was the perfect family for you to be born into in order to live the lessons that you needed to learn here on planet Earth. Remember that you made soul contracts with them! (Not with their issues, but with *them.*) You chose them to give you the exact human experiences you requested, and they chose you for the same reason. Any issues you have around them are a natural product of this loving agreement, but the issues are there for you to resolve, not to carry forever. I am clear on why I chose my parents in this lifetime. The gift of becoming who I was meant to become was only possible through the experiences I had with them. Being on the other side, I am truly grateful.

So what can you do about this? How do you stop getting triggered?

ASK YOURSELF

Whenever a difficult feeling or trigger comes up, think about *where* this feeling comes from. Most of the time, you'll realize that what you're carrying is something you learned from others whom you are mimicking. So what are you mimicking, and who showed you how to do that? List what you are feeling, then ask yourself: "Is it mine?"

- If you feel anger, ask: "Is this mine?"
- If you feel fear, ask: "Is this mine?"
- If you have anxiety, ask: "Is this mine?"
- If you feel vulnerable, ask: "Is this mine?"
- If you lack self-confidence, ask: "Is this mine?"
- If you lack self-esteem, ask: "Is this mine?"
- If you feel unlovable, ask: "Is this mine?"
- If you have money issues, ask: "Is this mine?"
- If you have relationship issues, ask: "Is this mine?"
- If you have food issues, ask: "Is this mine?"
- If you have body image issues, ask: "Is this mine?"
- If you have sexual issues, ask: "Is this mine?"
- If you have trust issues, ask: "Is this mine?"
- If you have issues with ego, ask: "Is this mine?"

If the answer is no, then lovingly give those issues back to whomever loaned them to you. Literally use your hands to push that big ball of energy away from you, and in your mind's eye see the person who gave it to you lovingly take it back, as it was never meant for you to hold. Chances are, your parents did the best they could, but because of their own trauma, they didn't have the ability to give you the full presence and loving-kindness you needed.

BONUS EXERCISE: *If you would like to experience an inner child guided energetic release exercise, please visit joliedawn.com/esf.*

Trigger Diffusion

As with many of the issues we're discussing in this book, solving the problem of triggers starts with awareness. It starts with shining a light on a blind spot so you can invoke the power of your choice in the situation. No awareness, no choice.

During my time in healing rituals with the enlightened master, I was able to give everything back that didn't belong to me. I gave back the insecurity, the religious confusion, the judgment, the rebelliousness. And I came out of that experience a much clearer version of who I actually was.

The giving-back process I went through in the healing retreat involved using props as symbols representing the energies of our parents that we were holding and that we wanted to return. In my case, I held a mirror that represented my mom's vanity and an empty wallet that represented my dad's money story. A woman acted as my mom, and a man acted as my dad, and I physically returned the items to them. This kind of therapeutic healing is sometimes referred to as "family constellations."

It really doesn't matter what props you use when you do this at home. You can just use your hands and make a pushing motion while you envision the energy returning to whoever gave it to you, or you can use physical props if that helps you make it more real. It's totally up to you.

There's such freedom to be found in doing this. Not only does it allow you to let go of your parents' issues and stop mimicking them, but it also places you in a space of gratitude to the people who brought you into this world. (This is true even if the people who gave birth to you didn't raise you, even if your dad or your mom was never a part of your life.)

This exercise lets you return what you don't want without anger or blame. Instead, you can recognize that you got to share in the human experience because of your parents. Giving back their issues with love and compassion will enable you to find that peaceful space.

To take the process a step further, I encourage you to create a visual timeline of your childhood. Check in with the little girl who is you through the years, from birth to adulthood. Start looking at all the pieces. What happened when, and how does it still affect you now? Note any major traumas, what you were dealing with, what really upset you, and whether you feel you have healed from those traumas.

ASK YOURSELF

I invite you to take some time now to bust out your journal, get quiet, go within, and write and reflect on the questions below.

- What's showing up in your life right now that isn't yours?
- What did your parents unintentionally hand you that you didn't want then and don't want now?
- How are you repeating struggles from the past?
- In what ways is the hurt little girl within you still running the show?
- What did it feel like to be you as a child?
- What is left unhealed?
- What is left unsaid?

- When you look back to the past, what are you very uncomfortable with?

So you may be saying, "Cool, now I know that I have triggers, but what do I do about them?" Fear not, sister. I have a simple four-step solution for you: be aware, allow, identify, and choose.

1. Be Aware of Your Triggers

Being aware of your triggers will enable you to reclaim your power. Let's say, for example, you get news that your best friend from high school didn't invite you to her wedding. Instantly, your body feels contracted, tight, heavy, and so on. It feels so natural to jump right into two responses:

- BLAME HER OR MAKE HER WRONG. As in: "What a bitch! She sucks! This isn't fair! She's so ungrateful! How dare she!"
- VICTIMIZE YOURSELF. As in: "What did I do wrong? I must have done something wrong. How could she do this to me? Why does this always happen to me? I guess I'm not worthy of the friendship. Maybe she never liked me at all."

Do either of those responses make you feel empowered? I doubt it. Instead of diving into either one, try simply standing in awareness of the trigger. Pause, breathe, and recognize the trigger as just that: an activation based on something that happened to you in your past. Be curious, without judgment.

Allow it to be just as it is. You could even say to yourself, with full awareness and interest, "I have been triggered."

2. Allow Yourself to Feel It

It is biologically ingrained in us to seek pleasure and avoid pain, so it will feel unnatural to stop and feel the unpleasant feelings triggers cause. Your body will yell at you to "*do something, damn it!*" This is its way of avoiding the pain of your trigger. It will try to get you to distract yourself, push the hurt down, or run away from it.

But feeling it is crucial. If you don't allow yourself to feel the discomfort of the trigger, it will become stuck in your energy field and just keep coming back up again. As soon as you notice that moment of heaviness, whether it's from feeling left out, betrayed, hurt, disappointed, stressed, annoyed, angry, confused, grieving, ashamed, embarrassed, or whatever it is, open up to it. Allow yourself to feel all of it.

Here are a few possible ways to lean into this discomfort:

- STOP AND RECOGNIZE WHAT IT FEELS LIKE IN YOUR BODY. Where is the feeling located? What parts of you does it impact? How?
- GIVE IT A VISUAL OR TACTILE QUALITY. Does it have a color? Shape? Texture?
- FIND WHAT EMOTION IT PROVOKES IN YOU AND EXPRESS THAT EMOTION TO YOURSELF. Scream, cry, pout, moan, swear — whatever you feel led to do. Don't label or think about the emotion; just feel it and express it from there.
- BREATHE INTO IT. Whatever the feeling is, focus deep breaths on it for at least a minute.

You might find other methods that work well for you. Just make sure the feeling doesn't cause you to fall into blaming or self-victimizing and don't distract yourself from it, hide from it, or bury it.

3. Identify a Time in the Past When You've Felt This Way

This is an important step in tracing your trigger back to its origin. So your friend didn't invite you to her wedding. You immediately got upset, but you've paused, used your awareness to identify the trigger, and breathed and felt into it. Now, have you felt like this in the past? That feeling of being left out, not good enough, or betrayed? What's your earliest memory of feeling like this?

Maybe the wedding scene that you're playing out is trying to get your attention in order for you to heal a past sisterhood wound. But there could be a completely valid reason for your friend not having invited you that you are totally missing. The trigger is now right in your face to show you that being left out is your story, not necessarily what is actually happening. Why are you so quick to make it about something she or you did wrong? Because it's really about something else. Look back. Note all the times you felt like this. When was the first time?

Or maybe a trigger has come up for you around a person you want to date not texting you back. You immediately feel unworthy, you start questioning your beauty, and you jump to blame. When do you first remember feeling like this? Maybe with your first boyfriend or girlfriend? Maybe with your dad or mom? Remember: this trigger that is surfacing now is showing you something that you never healed from in the past. This is your chance to play the detective. What is the trigger trying to show you? Root it out!

Recently, I realized that I avoided eating alone like the plague. It made me anxious to sit alone and eat by myself. I was curious about this and wanted to change it, so I thought back to my earliest memory of having anxiety when eating alone. Of course, it was in school! Eating alone meant you had no friends; you were a loner, an outcast. I carried this anxiety with me into my adult life; even though I was in completely different circumstances, my memories of feeling that way had stayed with me. Once I allowed myself to feel the discomfort and remembered its source, I knew why it bothered me so much. With that realization, I was clear for the last step.

4. Choose a Loving Story

If you're upset and you don't want to feel that way anymore, then how *do* you want to feel? There's no point in wasting precious life energy on something you aren't enjoying. Maybe you'd rather be peaceful, empowered, confident, and relaxed. With the wedding example, maybe you'd rather feel loved instead of hurt. Or maybe you want to be brave and compassionate enough to call the friend and tell her how you feel *without* blaming her or playing the victim.

Now allow yourself to release the old feeling...and choose your new, more preferred one.

You may be saying, "Jolie, is it really that easy? Just choose? What if I can't?" Yes, it really is that easy. Once you have the awareness that you are triggered, it's up to you to make the choice. Choose to tell yourself a loving story. I know that sometimes it can be challenging to feel joy in the middle of an anger trigger. You may choose to experience anger, and that's okay. Remember step 2! You have to feel it before you can let it go. But once you've felt it, don't hang on to it. You don't ever have to hang on to anything that hurts you. You are in the driver's seat of your emotional experience. This is where your empowerment lies.

In my case, I was anxious about eating alone, but I actually wanted to feel chilled out, confident, and present during the experience of eating a delicious meal. When I realized that I was operating from a past fear, I was able to put the fear to rest and make a conscious choice to enjoy the wonderful "me time" I had whenever I got to eat alone.

See, unresolved past experiences — triggers — keep you from choosing how you want to feel in every moment, but only as long as you let them. What feels like you're being hijacked is actually an opportunity to understand yourself better and grow from the knowledge. Are you willing to let yourself feel good? To have the courage to look within, feel it all, and create something new?

This four-step process will eventually become second nature to you. You will be able to observe your triggers instead of being consumed by them. With practice, soon you will have mastery over your emotions and find yourself rocking *any* heavy situation that may arise. Try using this process in your journal when you want to get over a sticky situation with ease and velocity.

You will often find yourself disempowered and lacking freedom if you let yourself be a victim of the past, and you will not feel very sexy if you are judging yourself all the time. I believe in you. You can do this! I know it can be really painful to dig up some of this stuff, but stay with it. Try to stay in the healing of you — not in the story your mind has made up, not in the trauma or drama, but right here, where you have an intention to clear it and move forward.

You are so brave for being the type of woman who is willing to do deep introspection. You are much more aware and intuitive than you give yourself credit for. You are destined for a future of joy, love, abundance, and ease if you choose it. Remember, this life experience can be paradise if you create it that way. The power is in your hands.

In the next chapter, we will examine the part that your ego plays in emotional hijacking and how you can have your ego work *for* you instead of against you.

CHAPTER FOUR

I Embrace My Ego

When I think of ego, I think of the little voice in my head constantly invoking worry, doubt, competition, and self-consciousness. I imagine it whispering sweet nothings like "You're not going fast enough — people are beating you!" The voice isn't always fun, as it creates fear. It tells us to do more, acquire more, stand out more, prove more. It's on the hunt for significance, prestige, attention. It's a thief of the present moment, making us focus on the past or the future.

Maybe you've used the word as an insult: "He has such a big ego!" "She's so egotistical!" People with a big ego are typically seen as rude or as caring too much about how they look, what they own, or how good they are at something (or everything!). They use the word *I* a lot. They don't listen so much as they wait to get to talk. They consider themselves the most interesting people in the room, and whether they admit it or not, they think they are better than most people. These days, we might call them narcissists.

Even the way we discuss the ego shows our distaste for and fear of it. We talk about fighting the ego, killing it, destroying it — or at least keeping it from getting too big or taking over. We walk on eggshells around the ego — our own and other people's — and whenever we can, we try to escape it. When we drink or get high and say we are getting stoned, smashed, destroyed, or annihilated, we are talking about escaping the ego. The alcohol or other substances we take silence the ego's terrible voice for a few precious moments. Suddenly our dancing is amazing, our creative expressions are masterpieces, and everyone is beautiful.

But what is the ego, really? Was some big mistake made when humans were created? Is it just a malfunctioning part on the human assembly line?

Actually, this superficial view of the ego isn't what the ego is at all. The ego isn't "bad." It's not something to fear or escape from, and having an ego is not the same thing at all as being a narcissist. In fact, your ego wants to be held, loved, and put in check with clear boundaries.

The website Dictionary.com defines *ego* as: "The 'I' or self of any person; a person as thinking, feeling, and willing, and distinguishing itself from the selves of others and from objects of its thought." In other words, the ego is simply your sense of self or your self-concept. It is the intellectual understanding of who you are. It's the you that operates in the world and interacts with other people. You can make conscious decisions about how your ego operates.

Here's what I know to be true about the ego.

The ego is a crucial part of human greatness. Our ego reminds us what we are capable of. It gives us that little push when we're being lazy. It helps us realize our full potential. We must learn to work with the ego, not against it.

The ego is actually a strong positive force! It is the drive that allows humans to constantly push beyond what we thought was possible, making each endeavor bigger and stronger than the previous one.

This point came to me clearly in New York City in my early twenties. I'll never forget the first time I stood on the observation deck of the Empire State Building and looked down at humankind's creation with sheer awe. Human egos drove us, encouraged us, and supported us in building that magnificent feat of architecture and the expansive city around it.

The ego has likely been a major driver in human evolution. But like anything else, when we put too much emphasis on it, it can grow out of proportion, turning into arrogance, selfishness, and, yes, narcissism.

On the other side, when we don't put enough emphasis on our ego, it can shrivel up and take all our self-confidence and ambition with it. We can lose a sense of our own identity. Like all the other parts of us, the ego works in our best interest when it exists in a balanced state. You need the ego to live in the world and function within a society and with other people, but you also need to see it for what it is and pull back when it becomes overactive or when you spend too much time focusing on yourself and not enough time looking out for others and recognizing the deeper, more universally connected parts of yourself.

In short: your ego is your identity, and there is nothing inherently bad about your identity. But this isn't as simple as it sounds. How do you balance your identity with all that you need to do in this world, spoken and unspoken, conscious and unconscious? How do you let go of your ego when you are too attached to it, and how do you find yourself again when you lose yourself? To answer these questions, I'll share some important stories from my past that I hope will help you discover some new things about yourself.

Transcending My Ego

My twenty-fifth birthday was just around the corner, and I thought it would be the perfect excuse to rent a place away from home and spend some time connecting and healing with my mom. I've never seen a spirit shatter into a million fragmented pieces like I saw in my mother the day my dad committed suicide. Even though their relationship was incredibly tumultuous, they were each other's true loves, and she felt lost without him. Our pain had caused us to drift apart instead of closer together, and I had had enough of it. I was scheming a plan for big healing. I proposed the idea to her: "Hey, how about I rent us a suite in Hermosa Beach and we have a weekend together for my birthday? What do you say?"

She was delighted by the idea but asked if I could really afford it. I told her that yes, it was my treat! I had found the perfect place right on the boardwalk, with sliding glass doors that opened to the ocean!

And, unbeknownst to my mom, I had a plan. It involved our taking a psychoactive substance that would rapidly increase serotonin and dopamine to the brain.

Before I go on with this story, let me explain something important and relevant. As you might know, in the last few years there has been a lot of research about how psychedelic substances can create breakthroughs for people with depression, anxiety, and other mental health issues. It's controversial (although becoming less so), but what's really interesting about these medicines is that they can help people temporarily separate from their egos. For many, the feeling of separateness and sense of self dissolve. In neuroscience, this phenomenon is called "ego dissolution," and it can create big breakthroughs in self-awareness and an understanding of the unity of all things.

That may sound contradictory: How can you become more aware of yourself if you dissolve your identity? What these substances do is give you an elevated understanding of who you are deep within (your soul), undistracted by who you are on the surface (your ego). With all the issues I had with my mother and with all the grief and trauma we had both been going through since my father's death, I decided (in all my "wisdom") that my mom and I needed to have this experience together, so that we could rise above our petty external egos and find our common ground and soul bond again.

I was young and full of big ideas, and I had been doing a lot of experimenting with these drugs and experiencing my own breakthroughs. I could see how stuck my mom was, and I wanted us to come back together, or maybe come together in a more meaningful way for the first time. Sharing a psychoactive experience with her was how I thought I could make that happen.

Before we left, I gave her a casual sneak preview of what was to come. I told her, "So one other thing. My friend gave me these pills that increase your dopamine and serotonin in the brain. I already have tried them, and they are great. Will you take them with me?"

My mom agreed. "Sure, honey! That sounds great. It actually sounds like something I probably need to take every day!"

I smiled. "Well, it's not exactly a daily kind of supplement, but it will make us feel great while we're on our vacation. Let's take them on the evening of my birthday!"

She was so excited to go on a vacation with me that she agreed to everything. I felt that a "Don't ask, don't tell" approach was best — for whatever reason, she wasn't asking exactly what we were taking, so I decided not to tell. Having said that, I in no way recommend that anyone else should ever dose another person without that person's full knowledge. This situation was unique: my religious, straight-edged mom, who had rejected *all* drugs in the 1970s (even though she was always around them) because she was too pure to do such things, had just consented to take a psychoactive journey with me. I knew this experience would do wonders for our relationship. I planned to give her a full dose. None of this half-dose, half-in bullshit. We were going to go all the way together.

Before the trip, I called up a friend and got us the best and the purest kind you can get. My friend told me that she and her boyfriend had done a ritual night with it and that two capsules was the perfect dose. I packed my bags. I was ready.

On June 9, 2014, my mom and I drove about two and a half hours up the coast of California, from San Diego north to Hermosa Beach. We jammed, listened to music, and chitchatted about people we knew. I didn't want another superficial weekend of shopping, eating, drinking, and sharing her occasional Marlboro Lights 100s. I wanted more. I was determined that this weekend would be different.

We got to the hotel, found the right suite, and opened the door. The wow factor was huge. Big, spacious, and luxurious, the room was on the ground floor, as close to the ocean as we could get. It was perfect. We spent the evening settling in and grabbing dinner before my birthday the next day. Nobody has ever been able to trigger me like my mom, so I took it slow with her, being as patient and as present as possible. I kept telling myself: "Be calm. Be present."

We woke up on my birthday and enjoyed an ocean-breezy, relaxed brunch. Today was the day. At four o'clock in the afternoon, I brought out the baggie. I dropped four capsules into my palm and held it out: two for her, two for me. We clinked them together as if saying, "Cheers!" I handed her a glass of water, and we swallowed them.

She. Fucking. Swallowed. Them.

I had no idea what was going to happen next, but I thought we probably needed to go outside, so I said, "Let's go for a walk on the boardwalk. We'll have about forty-five minutes before this kicks in and we feel anything, so let's go move and enjoy the sunshine."

We walked down the Hermosa Beach boardwalk and over to the pier, pretty far from the hotel. I began to worry. My mother was sixty-four, not in great health, and a full dose of psychoactive medicine was making its way through her bloodstream. She was about to get hit with a ticking time bomb. Forty-five minutes passed, and we were still about a ten-minute walk from our suite when we both felt it come on at exactly the same moment.

"Whoa," my mom said. "I feel really dizzy. I don't know if I can walk. I need to go back to the room."

Panicking inside but sounding calm, I said, "Yes, we're already headed back. Nothing to worry about. We'll be there soon. Just keep breathing. You're okay."

Suddenly I felt like my entire body was caught in a huge Hawaiian wave. I was rolling with the pulse of the planet, blasting off into a journey. And I, unlike my mom, at least understood what was coming.

We made it back to the room, but then my mom began to panic. "*Jolie, what the hell did you give me??*" She put her head in her hands and crouched over.

"Mom, just breathe," I said. "If you panic, it won't be fun."

Suddenly I knew what I had to do. I turned on my Bluetooth speaker and put on happy music. I busted out the bottle of flavored sparkling water in the fridge and two flutes. I poured us each a glass and put a big smile on my face. "Mom! It's my twenty-fifth birthday! Have fun with me! It's fun! *Have fun with me!*" I handed her the glass, and she looked at me. I could see in her eyes that she realized she was on a ride she wouldn't be able to get off for a while. She could either buckle up and go with it or resist it. I saw the surrender on her face. She focused all her energy to come back to me — to show up for her daughter's birthday. I loved her so much in that moment.

We toasted and enjoyed our drink like it was our last day on earth together.

Over the next thirty minutes, we both learned to dance with this medicine. It was big and all-consuming. I wondered how it would have gone if we had each taken only one pill, because the dose we took was strong and intense, but I decided to trust that it was the perfect dose. Over the course of the next few hours, we sat on the patio gazing at the ocean and smoking tobacco. After a while, she seemed to forget she was in an altered state. We were just simultaneously living in an altered dimension, the two of us there together, and we had each other. We really fucking had each other. We felt connected. For me, it was sweet, intense, weird, awkward, anxiety inducing, and also surprisingly calming.

As the sun started to set, I suggested that we leave the nest.

Changing the environment in a psychedelic journey completely changes the experience, altering the vibe. She felt nervous to move.

"Wait, leave our room? No! I'm comfortable here."

"Mommmmm," I whined. "It's my *birthday*. I want to see the sunset from the rooftop bar."

This turned out to be a smart move, to keep mentioning my birthday. It worked every time. "Okay," she said. "Let's go for fifteen minutes, then come right back."

We settled into a little corner of the bar and watched the sunset. It was a warm summer day, the perfect temperature, and it felt easy to relax there.

I suggested we go off to the side of the building, where we could be alone and share a cigarette. My mom was always down to smoke, so she was in. We were feeling good, and I felt that both our hearts were opening to love and peace. My plan was working.

I brought over two chairs for us. No one else in sight, just my mom and me, sitting there in the warm dusk of the summer evening. It was time to open my heart to her.

"Sooo...," I ventured. "I really wanted to have some time this weekend for us to get to know each other again, with all of our past behind us. Just you and me, mother, daughter, heart to heart."

"Okay...," she said, reluctantly. "Sure, honey. What is it?" I was disturbing her peace. I could see it. She was probably waiting for me to tell her something terrible! But I had to get this out of me.

"Here's what I want to say." I took a deep breath. "You know, my career is taking off. I'm becoming a powerful, successful leader for women. I'm speaking on stages. I'm telling my story, and people are loving it. I'm seeing momentum and success in my coaching business. And I'm making real money now."

I could see her relax a little, softening into listening, as if she was thinking, "Well, this isn't so bad."

I went on. "But I feel I haven't always done the best job of filling you in on what is going on in my life. I've been afraid you'll judge me if I tell you the things I'm excited about. I know that's ridiculous, because I know you're so proud of me and love me for me...right?"

"Of course, honey," she said. "You know I'm proud of you and your confidence. You're such a little go-getter."

"Aww, thanks, Mom. I love you so much, and I hope you know how much I deeply love, adore, and respect you, even though we may not see eye to eye on everything."

"I love you so much, too," she said, lapsing into her pet names, "my mushy burger, my honey bunches of oats, my beloved baby girl." There was nothing in our space together but pure, mutual love and acceptance. It was beautiful, real, indescribable love between a mother and a daughter. It was a bond that can never and will never be broken. It was soul deep, the love of the mother of creation. It was as vast as the cosmos and as abundant as the seas. We reveled in the love of each other. It was fucking adorable. My mom has always been a sharer. She loved to share about her memories and her childhood, so she began talking. "You know, Jolie, I never really knew if my mom loved me or not. I mean, I knew she loved me in an obligatory way, but I could never tell if she really *liked me* or *wanted me*."

"Mom, that's really sad. I didn't know you felt that way."

"My family life was hard. I never felt like I fit. I had shattered self-esteem that I never really recovered from."

I leaned in. This was something new. She went on to tell me

things I had always wanted to know about her, from how she lost her virginity to the guilt she'd never gotten over when her nephew committed suicide as a teenager.

"Mom!" I cried, trying to steer the ship. "Forgive yourself! It happened exactly as God planned. You have to trust that."

"You're the best daughter in the world, do you know that?" she said. "You're so fun and cool. I love that we can be doing this together, enjoying this moment together." Then she paused. "Wait…are you sure *this* is what you wanted to do on your birthday? Hang out with your old mom?"

"There's nowhere else I'd rather be," I said. "I wanted this to be exactly the way it is right now. I'll have a party with my friends when I get back."

She looked at me skeptically; even now, part of her doubted that I loved her and wanted her. But the medicine did help because in that moment I know she physically felt my love. That's the real power of this particular psychoactive. You really *feel things* again, no matter how long you've kept yourself from feeling. The experience transcends all time and space and memory. It's pure love medicine.

We began to giggle about life, and then she told me more stories. Finally, when she seemed to have let it all out, it was my turn again. I needed to finish what I'd started.

"Mom, can I tell you the real reason why my former fiancé broke up with me two months ago? I have to tell you, he and I weren't in a closed monogamous relationship." I swallowed. "Like…we were with other people when we were together."

My mom looked confused. "What do you mean, honey?"

"So…this medicine we're on right now? He and I did it for the first time together at a New Year's Eve party with all of our friends. At that party, we explored for the first time with other people. He had other women, and I had other people, too." I wasn't quite ready to tell her that I had been with other women that night. One thing at a time! "Our relationship was...un-conventional."

"Did other people know you were swingers?" She sounded concerned.

I couldn't help laughing at the word. "We weren't swingers, Mom. We just had an open kind of love. Some people call it polyamory, but we were just doing our own thing."

She nodded, unsurely.

"So...what I'm trying to say is, he broke up with me be-cause he had to. He could see that I wasn't in full romantic love with him, and let me tell you, I did plenty of things that made that clear, including not having sex for very long periods of time."

I was surprised to see my mom sigh with a kind of re-lief. "Honey, I'm actually really happy to hear this. I thought you were crushed and sad or full of anger or heartbreak. But you're not?"

"I'm genuinely not," I said. "In fact, I'm excited for my life as a young single woman. I never envisioned myself getting married until my thirties. Now I have so much time to be young and free. Plus I'll have more focus on my business."

I didn't get into all the details about how my ex was 100 percent supportive of my sexual exploration with women or how eventually it helped us both realize we weren't right for each other. What I really wanted her to know was, her idea that I had met the man of my dreams and we were the "it" couple of San Diego was wrong. It was my fault she didn't know the truth; I'd never been able to reveal it to her, because I was working so hard for her acceptance. I reassured her: "Mom, you don't have to worry about me. I don't need a man to provide for me. My business is making money, and it's just the beginning.

"And Mom…one more thing," I continued. "It's important for you to know this. I want to be free of the shame I'm carrying."

"Shame? Honey, why would you feel shame?" She reached for my hand.

I took a deep breath. "You know in high school, when I went to all those parties? I was really promiscuous. To be honest with you, sex was such a sin in our family and I felt so controlled that I rebelled, big time. And that rebellion ended up hurting me, a lot. In college, I wasn't safe. I'm still healing my body from that promiscuity."

"Honey! Why didn't you tell me?" she said. "I'm your mother! I'm here to love you no matter what!" She looked sad for me, sad that I'd hidden it from her, but also surprisingly calm. I think she was just happy I was telling her now.

"I'm handling it, Mom. I'm getting healthier every day. I'm proud that I'm not that girl anymore. I have boundaries. I've grown, and I make better choices. I'm even writing a book, and I'm mentioning some of this in it, so I don't want you to be surprised."

She hugged me, and I felt a huge release, a weight lifted off me. I no longer had to carry the burden of the lie. For the first time in my adult life, I felt authentic connection with my mom — no egos interfering, just truth and love.

"Wow," my mom said, after we sat in silence for a while. "I can see so clearly how many blessings God has given me in my life. I don't know why I lost touch with my gratitude. My life is abundant and beautiful, and I need to treat it like that. I have two beautiful, healthy, thriving children who love me. What more could I ask for? But honey, let me ask you one thing."

"What is it, Mom?"

"Do you really think we needed drugs to get here?"

"Mom, I believe we did. But what matters is that we're here, and now you know the parts of me I've been afraid to show you."

Mission accomplished.

That night was beautiful. Egos aside, identity aside, we got to love each other so purely. It was everything I had ever wanted and needed from her.

Fast-forward to four years later. After one lonely Sunday night, my mom didn't wake up from her sleep. She had wished her death upon herself since the day my dad left, and she was finally successful. The coroner later declared it to be heart failure. She literally died of a broken heart, and it makes me sad whenever I think of it. My first thought upon her passing was, "That's it? My relationship with my mom is over? That's all I get?" As I reflected on who I was to her as a daughter, I was proud. I never gave up on her. I did my best. I wasn't perfect, and I certainly could have been more loving at times, but I relentlessly showed up and took leadership in our relationship. Until the day she died, we never lost that new sense of intimacy and connection, and I don't believe we ever would have found it without being able to step away from our egos for one beautiful weekend.

As a young woman in her thirties who lost both her parents in her twenties, when I reflect on stories like this, I am so glad I did the hard thing and leaned into love to the best of my ability, despite having the desire to run from it at times. It is a true gift to not have any regrets. As irreverent as the above story may seem as a way of bonding with my mother, it was a huge milestone for us.

Finding the Lost Ego

Sometimes, you need to lose your ego to find your truth. But other times, you need to find your ego to have the strength to live your truth.

When I was twenty-two years old, I got a call from my boyfriend telling me to pack my bags and meet him at his entrepreneurs' retreat on Necker Island, aka Sir Richard Branson's private island in the British Virgin Islands.

You should know that Richard Branson is my absolute idol. Not only is he one of the most prolific living entrepreneurs in the world, the founder of the Virgin brand (Virgin Records, Virgin Mobile, the Virgin airlines) who now controls more than 400 companies in the Virgin Group, but he is also down-to-earth, adventurous, a philanthropist, and a cool dude in the sea of greedy, power-hungry mega-entrepreneurs of our day.

I knew for months that my boyfriend was going to be on this trip for seven days, and of course I wanted to go. He had tried, unsuccessfully, to pull strings to get me there earlier. But once he was there, he happened to mention me to just the right person, and she made it happen. I was elated! Not only was I going to Richard Branson's private island, but I was going to get to sit with him at the dinner table!

When I arrived at the tiny airport of the British Virgin Islands, it was the middle of the night and pitch black. I boarded a small speedboat, and off we went, blazing into the abyss of the sea. I was exactly where I needed to be, so free, so wild, so connected to the magic of life.

The boat took me to Branson's catamaran, the largest ever built. I thanked the man who had picked me up, then I boarded the catamaran and crawled into bed with my boyfriend.

The next morning, I was introduced to the other guests.

Little did I know that one of them would change my life. Over breakfast and a latte, I met her. Her name was Lindsay.

As we began to talk, I immediately felt accepted and at home — even though I was as far from home as I could imagine, in the middle of the Caribbean, on Richard Branson's boat, surrounded by the bluest waters I'd ever seen, with turtles swimming by. It was surreal, and I did my best to pretend that I deserved to be a part of it. But with Lindsay, I felt like I didn't have to pretend.

She told me that she was the only woman on the trip who wasn't a partner of one of the men; they had all subsidized her trip because she was such a lovely addition to the group. She was breathtakingly beautiful, with piercing blue eyes and the most adorable auburn freckles. Blonde, beachy-wavy hair, perfect teeth, full, naturally rosy lips, a gorgeous figure, and a warmth that made me feel like I was important and loved. Her smile was simple and pure.

I couldn't help guessing more about her. I imagined she was about thirty-five, led a wildly privileged life, was über-successful, and had everything handed to her. Surely, I thought, she's already had sex with at least one of the men here to earn her way. (Such was my thinking in those days.) Isn't it amazing what we can make up about someone before we know them?

She told me that she had just returned from a mission to India, where she had raised money for a reusable water bottle project and had hand delivered water bottles to kids at an orphanage. She'd flown directly from India to Necker Island with one suitcase. I was impressed.

I asked her what had inspired her to do such a thing. She said she lived for philanthropy. She'd already been on dozens of trips to the most poverty-stricken parts of the world in an effort to make a difference. She explained that she grew up with a mom addicted to meth and other hard drugs; her mother was homeless. She never wanted kids to feel rejection the way that she had. She also told me that she was twenty-two! She was exactly my age and already had three businesses. One of them was her blog, livemorehappy.com. She had left college to travel the world alone and learn about new cultures.

I was smitten. How had a woman my age already done so much? She was raw and roughed up by life, but yet she was a humanitarian. She had trauma and pain like I did, and yet look at what she had made of her life! We were instant friends. I remember saying to her: "You're an absolute miracle. You need to tell your story!"

Over the next few years, we collaborated in several ways. She spoke multiple times at the live Inner Goddess Unleashed Summit events I hosted in San Diego. She became a part of my early coaching program, the beginning of my women's work and entrepreneurship circles. She took me to the Door of Faith Orphanage in Mexico, where she had fundraised to throw the orphanage a party with a bounce house, piñatas, cakes, and art projects, and brought thousands of dollars' worth of supplies with her.

I watched her start the nature reserve program on Necker Island and have casual text convos with Sir Richard. I watched her work alongside other top global entrepreneurs and CEOs. I watched her soar in her career with LMH Promotions and enjoy the most exclusive invites, like artist passes to Coachella.

And yet the strangest thing about Lindsay was that she seemed to have no ego at all. There was no sense of accomplishment, no pride, no arrogance. She didn't appear to know how beautiful she was or how much of an impact she was making. It was almost like she didn't quite believe she existed. For all her gorgeousness and all she'd done for others, it was as if when she looked in the mirror, she saw nothing there.

Through the years, we developed a deep friendship. I knew what it felt like to have the world think you're amazing and successful but to feel empty and broken on the inside. I knew what it felt like to be judged as a ditzy blonde and to have to prove your intelligence and value.

When I self-published an earlier version of this book in 2015, I asked her to be a partner in my launch. On June 1, 2016, she wrote this about it on her blog, a post she called "Empowered, Sexy & Flawed":

> My dear friend Jolie Dawn just featured me as an "Empowered, Sexy & Free" woman in her book re-launch. It feels inauthentic when I look at it because I have not felt any of those things lately. Who am I to be featured? How fitting, though, that Jolie was one of the key people who pushed me to begin writing more openly and honestly. So here I am, challenging myself to share myself, to once again feel empowered and free.
>
> It's been very hard to write lately.
>
> I take that back.
>
> It's been very hard to share lately.
>
> Not only because I have been so busy with my new project, a renovation of a rundown beach house in Baja into a vacation rental, but for many reasons. *My spirit has felt broken.* I feel like I have suffered some serious losses lately.
>
> I lost my passion project business, Givebackpackers, to a lovestruck, obsessive computer programmer that stole the company by creating a competing website with the same name, to force me to work with him.

I've been harassed by this "friend" who wanted more than friendship for months now, causing me to fear for my safety and my security.

I lost my boyfriend of a year because of his health issues and have felt like I am constantly defending our mutual decision to people who just don't understand how "love just wasn't enough."

I lost a lot more money than I anticipated on this Mexico house, discovering that everything from the floors, kitchen, and windows to the plumbing and electrical needed to be completely replaced before even beginning to furnish [it].

Besides just money, I have lost time and faith. I've hired people who stole from me and who took advantage of my kindness.

I was unable to get the support of the neighborhood that I was expecting going into this project.

I've watched my stepmom's health struggle to return with more chemo than was expected, while my best friend is going through the same heartbreak of watching her mom fight cancer. It's been emotionally exhausting.

I am living in a constant state of defending myself, picking myself back up, and forcing a smile.

I'm a strong person because of everything that I have been through my whole life, [from] parenting myself from the time I was 5 years old to starting a business in a recession after dropping out of college to traveling the world alone.

There's so much I can face without fear, but being on the defense all the time is exhausting.

I can play offense. It's easy to be the one running down the field, but much scarier to have someone running at you.

I've defended my choices and my business, my house and my freedom. I've even had to defend my writing.

I've been hurt by the things people have said to me and behind my back. I've been tired of defending who I am, what I have created, and why.

I feel tired of defending and tired of being vulnerable. I want to shut it all down and hide away.

I'm afraid of being rejected or hurt any more. I'm afraid I won't be able to be strong through any more of it.

I'm a strong person, but I am sensitive. I know that I do not have to defend myself to the people who matter. I tell myself that the ones that matter already know me and love and support me, and the ones with whom I feel defensive don't matter.

I have held off for months sharing my writing and my thoughts. I have been biting my tongue to feel safe and supported. I have been seeking comfort and stability and ways to nurture myself.

I am writing and sharing this because I find strength in my honesty. I am not a fake person. I do not need to be adored by the masses and make everyone else feel comfortable at the expense of my own freedom.

So if you are reading this with anything but love, why are you reading?

If you are reading this with love and support in your heart, thank you. You are why I share.

As you can see, 2016 was a really hard year for Lindsay. I watched her mental health decline as it seemed that life kept letting her down. We went on a trip to Mexico together, and I remember having a hard time lifting her spirits. When I got home, I felt worried about her. How could she not see how amazing she was?

She shared openly on social media about her struggles in life, with men, with business partners, with friends. She had always had a positive message amid all the pain, but then I noticed that that started to change. I would reach out often to encourage her.

She was the friend who was there for me when my fiancé broke up with me. She told me I was young and hot and had the rest of my life ahead of me, so I should get excited, and it worked. I felt a surge of joy for life again in the middle of a terrifying life change. She always knew what to say.

I tried to be for her the person she was for me, but I always felt that she wasn't letting me very far in.

In the fall of 2016, I moved to Austin, Texas. It wasn't uncommon for us to lose touch for a few months at a time and then pick right back up where we'd left off. We were busy women. After I moved to Austin, we were out of touch for a period.

Then I answered a surprise FaceTime call from Lindsay's former business partner, who was a friend of mine. I was excited to say hello, but as soon as I saw her face, my mood changed.

She said, "Jolie, I just got a message from someone saying that Lindsay's body has been found."

I dropped the phone. I immediately felt sick. I called Lindsay, but her phone went straight to voicemail. Life came to a screeching halt, and I felt a pit of horror open in my stomach. I pleaded with God: "Let Lindsay be okay." But I knew she wasn't. I reached out to Susan, one of Lindsay's best friends, and she told me the harsh truth: "I was the one who found her. She was dead in her apartment when I broke in. She committed suicide."

One of my closest girlfriends in this life, gone in just an instant.

I kept thinking to myself, "How do I undo this? How can we get her soul back into her body? Surely she was out of her right mind; there has to be a way to fix this."

There was no fixing this one. No turning back. No redo.

Those gorgeous blue eyes, the freckled face, that contagious laugh, the perfection of her natural golden hair — it was all lifeless, about to be sent for cremation. I just kept seeing the image of her beautiful twenty-seven-year-old body wasted, thrown away. Sadness still pings me right in the center of my heart when I think about her.

During this time of massive loss, I questioned life more deeply than ever before. With my dad, it was different. Still terrible, but different. He had lived a full life, fought in the Vietnam War, left a legacy through his family. With Lindsay, so much more of the story was still left to be told. For the first time, I questioned my strong spiritual belief that "everything happens for a reason."

Her biological mother sent me her suicide note. It told the story of a woman who was rushing through life, far from who she had been before. If only we had seen it coming? Nobody had.

Lindsay had lost herself. She lost her identity in multiple relationships with men who cheated on her, in the pain of her childhood, in her desperate efforts to help others because she couldn't help herself. That beautiful soul left this planet while feeling absolutely worthless.

I reflected on all the times I had told her how much I valued her and what her worth was to others. These were the very things about her I was so envious of, and yet she'd never really believed them. After all those times she had helped me come home to myself, she wasn't able to come home to herself. And I wasn't able to help her. I felt guilty. I was inconsolable.

But I was alive.

Finding Balance

When you're spinning out, when you've forgotten who you are, or when you are so deeply involved with yourself that you don't see anybody else anymore, your ego is out of balance. How do you get back into sync with yourself and into that natural flow of identity in balance with connection? Egos can be complex, and you can't just snap out of it or fix it in a day, but here are my top three go-to ways to begin the process of reconnecting with the self, finding a home within, and working toward a clear vision of where you are and who is important in your life.

1. Come Back to Sacred Self-Love

The one theme that has been present in my life during every relationship and every breakup has been my forgetting to take care of myself. It's far too easy to lose yourself in another person and to forget how precious and vital taking care of your body and spirit is. It's also hard to see, when you think you are self-involved, how careless and cavalier you can be with your own body and soul.

At the start of each new day, I ask myself this question: "How can I best love myself today?" I wake up earlier, spend more time in nature, journal every day, and am hyperaware of opportunities to experience pleasure. I revisit interests I've put on the back burner. I listen to the inner voice of that little girl I once was, who deserves to be heard but who isn't sure she is worthy. I love myself more, not less. I am more patient with myself, not less.

ASK YOURSELF

Who are you? How well do you know yourself? Be curious about who you are, where you are, and what's going on within. Ask yourself:

- What do I know I deserve in this life?
- Where am I selling myself short?
- Am I unconsciously running from myself?
- Am I hiding in a partnership?
- Am I pondering a transition?
- What do I do that makes me lose track of time?
- What would I do all day long if I had the time and space?
- What turns on my being and lights me up?

Whatever you are going through, whatever you need, whatever you love, I urge you to prioritize *you*. Your lightness matters, your pleasure matters, and your daily self-care matters. Don't abandon your hurt inner child. Nurture and love her. She deserves it . . . and that means you do, too.

2. Do Something Every Day
to Raise Your Vibration

Energy is this fascinating phenomenon on planet Earth. We can't see it, but we know it exists. We can't perceive the solar rays hitting our skin, but we are certain if we stay in the sun too long, we will get burned. This is how caring for our own human energy works. It doesn't always feel like a priority to feed our spirit and choose friends and experiences that raise our vibration, but it all matters.

It's far too easy to forget how important it is to value ourselves. To have a fierce relationship with boundaries and say no when we mean no. To politely decline hanging out with that one friend who always drains our energy. To say, "Enough" when it's time to end a relationship. All of these small daily decisions matter. They make up the holistic vibration of you, and they're far too easy to forget to carry out.

Boundaries have always been a challenge for me. I couldn't say no when I was tired but friends wanted me to do something. I would say yes to the girls' Vegas trip when I knew I didn't want to drink for four days straight. I found myself in countless situations I didn't want to be in because I couldn't say no.

Another interesting human phenomenon is the aura. Lexico.com defines our aura as "the distinctive atmosphere or quality that seems to surround and be generated by a person, thing, or place." Learn about auras — learn about *your* aura. Take care of your aura. Go outside and get sun. Pause to reflect on life. Take up a journaling practice to process your emotions. Choose to hang out with friends who feed your soul. Have spine-tingling orgasms with people who respect you. Say yes to the spontaneous adventure. Tell your mom you love her. Get excited about your travel Pinterest board. Try a new workout that challenges you. Look at yourself in the mirror daily and say, "I love you."

All these small choices add up to the brightest, lightest you.

3. Reconnect to the Divine

Talking about God brings up a lot of different emotions for people. I know that for me, personally, it was hard to use the word *God* when I spoke of the magnitude of creation, because the type of religious training I received taught me to fear God. I was told that he was some man up in the sky who was incessantly judging me.

Now I personally like to address the divine directly, and saying the word *God* feels a lot different than it used to. It's my version of what I know to be true for me and not something that was forced on me. It's what I've practiced for myself and not learned through another.

I think of the divine as the universal force field that holds everything together and is the source of the magic that is life: the cosmos, a baby growing in the womb, and the natural instincts that govern animal and human life. It's the glue, the order, the love. It's the thing that is the hardest to put into language. It must be felt and discovered by every single individual, in their own time.

How connected do you typically feel to divine realms? What I want to remind you to do here is reconnect with a practice that asks you to be in awe of the universe. Connect to the thing that brings you to tears because it makes you so grateful to be alive. Connect to that moment of feeling total love and acceptance. Remember that it is your right to take up space on the planet and live with purpose.

There is no right way to do this, and you cannot mess it up.

Connecting to the divine can happen in many ways: through prayer, meditation, walking in a quiet park, swimming in the ocean, yoga, chanting, reading tarot cards, being in sacred spaces, journaling, hiking, or simply being alone with yourself and listening.

My favorite way to connect is to pull out all of my oracle and tarot decks and ask my spirit guides for messages. I tune in, slow it way down, look for the subtle and metaphorical clues, and write down the messages I receive in my journal. I speak to myself in my journal as if it were the divine speaking to me: "Jolie, why do you doubt yourself, Precious One? After all that you've created, and you're letting this trip you up? Trust, relax, let go…we got you." This is just an example — I'm not asking you to do anything like this if you're not into that level of mysticism. Find what your thing is.

When life tosses us around, kicks us down, and has us questioning everything, it is the perfect time to be curious about what is beyond the human experience. Wherever you are right now, whether you're in the middle of a spinout or feeling grounded and happy, these three practices have the capacity to turn the spiritual dial all the way up. Your happiness, peace, and joy matter in the world. It matters that you find a home within yourself and have access to tools and resources to rebound your energy when you feel low. Learn who you are again. Embrace yourself. Love yourself. And connect to the world again. Find your ego and love it for what it is…and also for what it isn't.

We are all human. At some point we will all have to sit with the consequences of choices we wish we hadn't made and face the harshness that is life. We all have to encounter fear, guilt, sadness, and anger. But we don't have to stay in this place. That's where anxiety and depression live.

To the dear souls reading this, I urge you to be curious about what home feels like within yourself. I dare you to try a new way of connecting to yourself, your body, and the divine realms. I encourage you to start asking bigger questions of life. And I appreciate you for being here, reading this.

May we all find our way home to ourselves.

Ego Soul Contracts

I believe that each of us made a contract with our ego long before we came to planet Earth. We knew that the ego could serve us greatly. We asked it to be a crucial part of our daily lives — to be the self we choose to use in this life, with an energy within us that is constantly turned on. Then, we chose to forget that we made the contract and trusted that we would figure things out for ourselves in the course of our human experience.

Unfortunately, a contract that is never updated can become irrelevant or, worse, harmful. Imagine for a moment if the United States had never updated its contracts after it gained independence from Great Britain. That's what the Declaration of Independence was, you know: a contract. We made that shit *real* by handing Britain a document that basically said, "You are archaic, and you can't control us anymore." That document made America's independence a real thing. At the time it was exactly what our country needed.

But imagine if we hadn't updated it (or the laws based on it) since then? Black people would still be enslaved, women still couldn't vote, and first cousins could marry in Utah (but only after they're sixty-five years old — I'm not making that up).

This is what's happened with the contract you have with

your ego. You asked the ego to play a particular role a long time ago, it agreed, and you entered into a mutually binding agreement. But you've never gone back and said, "Hey, this is outdated. Let's move on to more relevant priorities." You forgot that you have the natural ability to train your ego to work with you instead of against you.

To give you an example of this, I'm going to share my ego contract with you. (I literally have a Google Docs sheet labeled "Contract with My Ego." Just like the Declaration of Independence, this puts the terms of our agreement down on paper, where they can't be denied.) I'm especially eager to share with you some of the terms in my contract that I forgot to update for about fifteen years — long past when they needed a refresh. I believe my original request to my ego was to show me what people were creating around me so that I could be inspired by them. I wanted to compare myself to other people in order to have a point of reference, but because I hadn't updated my contract in so long, my ego was running wild!

It had me:

- valuing material possessions way too much as a way to measure how "successful" I was
- feeling the need to exaggerate my accomplishments so as to make myself feel worthy
- playing out all the possible scenarios in my head about how I would run out of money, become homeless, and let my family starve

All that ego was making me feel like shit! So I decided to make a new contract — one that would serve me as I am now rather than as I was before.

Here is my new and updated contract.

Contract with My Ego

I, Jolie Dawn, unconditionally love you, my ego. You have been doing exactly the job I asked you to do. Thank you, thank you for the perspective. I know you've been acting out of love to the best of your ability.

But now it's time for an upgrade, because our outdated terms are impacting my quality of life. I want to form a tight partnership, so I propose a relationship within which you work synergistically with my higher mind.

Here are the things I would like you to let go of doing to redefine our relationship:

1. **COMPARING MYSELF TO OTHER PEOPLE.** Thank you so much for being on the lookout, showing me where I can improve and what else is possible. I no longer desire to use you to compare myself to other people, because now this makes me feel less than them and bad about myself. Instead, I would like to celebrate others' successes and see their wins as my wins. Can we agree to this?

2. **FEARING ABOUT MONEY.** I know you're just trying to protect me, keep me safe, and make sure I'm taken care of, but my concern about money has gotten out of hand. It seems like I can never earn enough to make you feel comfortable. I would love for you to alert me when I am being grossly irresponsible with money or if it really looks like I'll end up homeless on the streets, but until then, I've got this. I live in the abundance-mindset paradigm now, and I would like you to work with me in that space. Instead of being on alert for all the ways I might run out of money, can we

please use that energy to create more money together?
Let's redirect that energy to expand more and attract
more opportunities.

3. **JUDGING MYSELF FOR NOT CREATING FAST ENOUGH.**
    I know you're trying to motivate me and keep me pro-
    ducing at my best, but let's work with the higher mind
    to remember that everything is unfolding in divine
    timing. There really is no rush.

4. **THINKING SOMEONE ELSE'S WIN TAKES AWAY FROM
    MY WIN.** Even though my former fiancé hired my
    roommate to run his company — the company that
    I felt so much a part of while we were together — this
    doesn't mean that nausea and distress need to take over
    my entire body. Look, I know your intentions are good;
    you really want me to be safe and have the best. But
    someone else winning does not mean that it takes away
    from my wins. The reality is that this is an abundant
    universe, and there is more than enough for everyone.
    I truly win when everyone wins. Please work with my
    higher Self to celebrate other people's wins.

5. **KEEPING MYSELF FROM ENJOYING THE PRESENT
    MOMENT.** Yes, I know a large tax bill came to me today,
    significantly higher than I was expecting, but it doesn't
    mean that I need to be in a bad mood, judge myself,
    and let it ruin my day. Please align with the knowing-
    ness of my higher mind, so that I can see how every
    "problem" has a gift inside it. This is all unfolding per-
    fectly, and *I'm okay*. Thank you for alerting me. If mo-
    ments of shock arise, please work with my higher mind
    to allow presence, ease, confidence, and beauty to fill
    me internally, no matter what is happening externally.

6. **FEELING THE NEED TO EXAGGERATE MY SUCCESS.**
   I've noticed that in conversation, I feel the need to prove myself in order to feel worthy. I've found myself exaggerating what I have created in the past, with the intention to have another person feel like I'm the real deal — like I've made it. I realize now that I do not need to do this. I am already enough. What I've accomplished is enough. I believe in myself. Instead of interjecting in conversations to remind me of what I need to prove, please, from now on, let me speak in truth. Allow me to let go of the desire to make anyone think anything but what's real about me. I am committed to living in my fullest authenticity, and I would like your support with that.

   Signed *Jolie Dawn*

   Signed *Jolie's Ego*

A contract like this is truly an incredible tool to use in moments of fear, anxiety, stress, and doubt. As you saw in section 4 of my contract, just a few months before I wrote it, my former fiancé hired my roommate to run his company. I literally felt like I was dying. I had forgotten to update the contractual term about what other people's wins meant for me. When I opened my document and wrote, "I truly win when everyone wins," I immediately felt a huge sense of relief.

Now I invite you to create your own contract with your ego. What terms are begging for you to update them? Maybe you're dealing with jealousy of an ex and need to create a term saying, "Nobody has the power to diminish my worth." Or maybe you are feeling the anxiety of not having enough money and need to create a term like "My bank balance and self-worth are two separate measures." You know inside what terms are not working for you.

My invitation now is to open a Word or Google Docs file and create your own contract with your ego. You can use my example as a template, but your content should be your own, based on your own needs. Take some time to really figure out what you are feeling the most resistance to in your life right now, then use that insight to create at least five updated terms in your contract with your ego. You'll be surprised at the greatness that lies on the other side of your fears.

I hope you are now beginning to see that even the things you think are "bad" or "wrong" about you are actually meant to help you grow. You are more magical and brilliant than you've ever given yourself credit for, and your ego is here to support you. It just needs to know what you need *today*; it needs some boundaries set by a loving authority.

Coming up next, we will examine how the words you speak create your reality and how making a shift in language will shift everything you create in your life. Let's do this!

CHAPTER FIVE

I Speak My Life into *Existence*

anguage. We use it incessantly but rarely take the time to examine what we're saying. After all, *spelling* contains the root *spell*, as in "to cast a spell." What spells are you casting with your language? Are you aware that you're speaking your life into existence by the words you use and the language you speak? Let me give you some examples.

When we talk about leaving a relationship, we say we had a "breakup."

When we describe not having money in the bank, we say we are "broke."

The word used to describe leaving a marriage is "divorce," which means "to break the marriage agreement."

We break bones, we break promises, we break appointments, we break contracts. Even when we're ready to stop working, we say we "need a break." Think about that. As human beings, we talk about breaks *all the time*. Why? Why do broken things show up in our language so often?

Because in some way, we all believe we *are* broken. We believe that we keep breaking everything around us. That something is deeply wrong with us and we will never be quite whole. Outwardly we may present a complete, perfect surface to the world, but our language gives us away. That surface is really a fragile, breakable shell.

Can you see how this is problematic? When we speak about being broken, we act as if we are broken. And when we embark on journeys to become whole, we start from this place of brokenness without realizing that we already *are* whole — and always were.

We come into the world as perfect beings. But somewhere along the way we picked up the belief that we are not. We bought into a lie that there is something about us we need to fix or change.

Is this where you are right now? Seeking, pursuing, searching, trying miracle solution after miracle solution, but never finding the wholeness you seek?

What are you really looking for?

Remembrance. We want to remember the divine perfection we started with. We want to remember that we can never be broken and we don't need fixing (even though it may feel that way, it just isn't true). You are a perfect, whole woman — be mindful if you're speaking about yourself as anything less than that.

So how *do* we remember? What can we do right now in our lives to stop the cycle of believing in our "brokenness"?

Here is the secret: you create it all with your language.

How you speak, your word choices, your stories — the words that come out of your mouth create the life you're living, your entire universe. The more you talk about breaking and being broken and being broke, the more broken you and your world will feel and appear. Like attracts like in this physical reality.

Our cave-dwelling ancestors had a very minimal range of words and therefore a very limited capacity to communicate feelings, problems, emotions, and so on. Today we have *over one million words* in the English language alone. We have a huge range of words to choose from to describe our lives. We can choose words that empower us or disempower us.

Here's another example: When I was transitioning out of my long-term relationship, the one thing that saved me from intense heartache was the *language* that we used when we spoke about it. I credit our language with allowing me and my former partner to create a solid friendship.

For example, we never said we were going to "break up." Instead, we said we were going to "transition" our relationship, because inside of "break up" is the notion that something is broken! There actually wasn't anything broken. We just realized that our romantic connection had become much more of a platonic relationship. We had even joked with each other that we were going to be that couple sleeping in separate bedrooms in five years! It was time for our relationship to transition. And I get it, sometimes breakups really do feel like something broke; I've had that kind, too. Even then, even when I'm hurt — especially when I'm hurt — I am mindful with my words and choose to create a narrative that empowers me.

My choice to speak this way doesn't mean I wasn't sad, and it doesn't mean I wasn't scared. But I was in touch with the reality that this change was best for me, and I purposefully chose language that supported that reality. It wasn't always easy. When I got on the phone with some friends, they unknowingly used language that made the transition into a big trauma:

"Oh my gosh, I don't even believe in love if you two can't make it!"

"What an asshole!"

"This must be so terrible!"

These wonderful women loved me and wanted the best for me. It would have been so easy to join them and say, "How could he do this to me? I really trusted him! This was a huge betrayal, and I feel hurt! I hate him!" But luckily, I had enough awareness not to get lost in that disempowering, heavy, contracting way of using language around what had happened.

I made the effort to keep coming back to my truth: "No, we're just transitioning our relationship." I never called him "my ex," just "my former partner." And by my (and his) choice to use that language, our transition remained smooth and positive, which allowed us to maintain and deepen our friendship even as our romantic connection ended.

This is the power that consciously choosing your language can have.

So how do you start making that choice?

It begins with awareness. I want to ask you to start looking at the language you choose to use, to really become aware of it. And as you start to cultivate the world of possibility, start to cultivate your language choices to match that world.

Example: Somebody you meet at the gas station says, "Oh, gas prices are so expensive! It's so hard to make money."

You might be able to reply, "Yeah, you know, I'm so grateful for all the transportation options in this city and happy that I get to have a car and drive at all!"

Example: A coworker says, "God, I hate my job so much."

You can say back to them, "I'm really appreciative of all of the experience I'm gaining here."

Do you see the power of that reframe of language? Don't buy into people's language of "Life is so hard" unless you're okay with living a life that's "hard." You can be the one to say something that will actually serve you, and you might make someone else think twice, too. It will take practice at first, but it will pay off, I promise.

The box below includes more examples of empowering ways to reframe your language.

Disempowering Language	Empowering Language
I can't do that.	I believe anything is possible.
I wish I could have that.	I will have that, and it's already on its way to me.
I'm in debt.	I am paying for past expenses.
I'm broke.	I am open to receiving more money.
We broke up.	We are transitioning our relationship.
I wish I had a different family.	I'm grateful for the lessons my family teaches me.
I am fat and ugly.	I am learning to love myself more deeply and fully.
I need to lose weight.	I commit to a routine to be healthier.
I should love myself more.	I choose to love myself every day.
I want to travel, but I have no money.	I challenge myself to find creative ways to travel inexpensively.

Here are a few tips about specific words and phrases to help you practice your positive, empowering language.

1. **"I AM"**: Be aware of what follows "I am…" That statement is very powerful. How often do you say things like "I am lazy," "I am tired," "I am fat," "I am a procrastinator," "I am shy," or "I am not good at…"? And then, guess what? You feel and act like you really *are* lazy, tired, fat, a procrastinator, shy, or not "good" at whatever thing you decided you weren't good at. Be aware of when you do this, and instead rock out some positive affirmations, like "I am magic," "I am abundance," "I am divinely guided," "I am amazing," "I am beautiful," "I am powerful," and "I am getting stronger / happier / more confident every day."

2. **"I WISH"**: Saying, "I wish…" will always keep you wishing. Instead of saying, "I wish I had that beach house," try, "I am so excited to create that for myself!" Cut the wishing out of your vocabulary. It's keeping you in a state of scarcity. You *do* have the power to create anything you'd like. Own it!

3. **"DEBT"**: The word "debt" carries such a heavy vibration. Rarely anyone ever says, "Yay, I love paying my debt!" Cut the word "debt" and use "past expenditures" instead. My greatest money mentor, Cory Michelle, taught me this one. It feels so much lighter to speak about paying off your past expenditures than about paying off debt — and it reminds you of the things those expenditures got you, things you can be grateful to have in your life or to have experienced.

4. **"TRY"**: When you say you are going to "try" to do something, that really means that you are not doing it. Either

you are doing it, or you're not. There is no try. So make a decision: either be a *hell yes* or be a clear *no*. We all know the friend who says, "I'll try to meet you guys!" — and she never comes. "Try" equals not doing it.

5. **"SHOULD"**: Oh boy, do we love our "shoulds"! Our obligations, our duties, our burdens, the things we're *supposed* to do. I wonder what your life would look like if you didn't do anything based on what you thought you "should" do. When you use the word "should," it implies that you are not accepting yourself or the situation *as it is*. The statement "I should eat healthy food" is full of resistance. Instead, say, "I am interested in creating a better diet for myself." See and feel the difference?

6. **"BUT"**: "I love you, *but* we are growing apart." "I want to go, *but* I have to work." "I think she's great, *but* she talks a lot." "I'm sorry, *but* you took my comment the wrong way." Notice how adding the word *but* completely negates the first part of the sentence. It cancels it out. If instead you say, "I want to go, *and* I have to work," your language opens a space for another possibility. Try using that substitution in a sentence, and notice how much lighter it feels.

My love, you came here for a purpose. You incarnated in the body that you have because you are meant to open magic portals with the gift of words, which are powerful and divine, and fulfill your destiny on the planet. The way that we understand our relationship to the divine is inextricably linked with how we think about and use language.

When you are spelling something, you are stepping into the magical powers of incantation, of charm. You are an enchantress, using your words to spin magic. *Abracadabra!* I love this word. It's what magicians say when they're waving their magic wands over the hat that's about to reveal a bunny or a flock of doves. Abracadabra: I create as I speak.

To look back at one religious tradition, in the book of John in the Bible, the first words are: "In the beginning there was the Word. The Word was with God, and the Word was God." Why was Word the very first thing in existence? Because words consist of sound vibrations that connect us to all that is. Some believe that when you speak words, you are creating vibrations that are forever recorded in the Akashic records, the universal "book" within which exists everything that ever was, is, and will be. This is how important words are! I believe words live in this time, space, dimension, and reality. They live as energy, and they're more powerful than we realize.

Would your business exist if you did not have language? Would your passions? Your relationships? Would anything that you do exist for you without language? In the classes I teach, the way I open and work with someone's consciousness is possible only because we have language. You can use words to perform magic. Just because we do it every day doesn't mean that it's not wildly profound. Without words, a thought couldn't become a reality. Without words, the world as we know it wouldn't exist. As mentioned before, words are essentially spells, and spells are the scripts to our existence.

Consciously Utilize the Power of Your Words

You have inherited a massive gift: to be born at this time and to have language and writing passed down to you. It's an absolute privilege to be able to read and write. For many centuries, common people weren't allowed to do it. Even after White women in the United States and other countries were allowed to be literate, many women of color were not. To read and write is to have power, and giving power to women has always seemed risky...to men.

As a literate woman who is reading this book right now, you have a huge advantage because your words and language are what form the power of speaking. You possess the massive opportunity to inspire those around you with your words and to be the creatrix of your most desired life through your use of language. Be the woman who intentionally uses this power. Speak beautiful visions into existence. Open your journal and write a beautiful story of the life and future you're creating. Start conversations with others that portray a world that works for everyone. Think beautiful thoughts of self-love and affirmation, and speak them out loud as often as you can. Use your voice to carry a transmission of hope, joy, and possibility. Use your voice as an instrument of change. Own your self-expression as a sacred duty. Vocalize your opinions and viewpoints as a holy act of leadership. Let this power of voice move as a vibration through your lips to reverberate out so the cosmos can feel your clear and willful intention. We are always creating the story of our lives either consciously or unconsciously — which do you choose?

I remember when the Covid-19 pandemic started to take hold in early 2020. My initial reaction was a lot of uncertainty and fear. I was hosting a retreat for twenty-two women in Southern California in mid-March when the president declared a national emergency. The future became very bleak in an instant. The dialogue both in my head and aloud sounded like: "It's all so unknown. This has the potential to really affect the economy and push us into a global recession. Will we have food to eat? Is this the end of my time as a successful entrepreneur?"

Then I woke up. "This is not me," I thought. "I refuse to start telling a disempowering story of my life, my business, and my future. The stakes are too high. My leadership is on the line." I used my voice to start speaking a new narrative into existence, and believe me, it was a conscious effort. It sounded like "no matter what happens externally, I am always safe with God and within myself. My freedom is not up for negotiation; that's an inside job that can never be threatened. No matter what happens in the economy, I trust myself as a resourceful woman, and I know I will always have my needs met. Faith is a full-time job — not just for when it's convenient or easy — and trusting the divine unfolding is a decree I live by."

If I had stayed in the downward spiral of fear, I would have created more fear around me and more doubt in my mind. It certainly would have affected my ability to lead in my business. I would have likely started conversations by listing all the potential ways life is unsafe and resonated more with the vibrational reality of fear. But I knew better than to entertain that bad dream. I am too committed to living a beautiful, expansive life than to let that happen for any significant period of time.

Instead, I went inward. I shut out the external noise and got really quiet within myself. My journal was once again my sacred place of processing my thoughts and feelings, and I talked to my higher self and God. What came from this was a massive step into my next level of leadership — the biggest leap in my eight years of running my business up to that point. A palpable power came over me. In the beginning pandemic days, when nothing made sense, I did my part to create an empowering conversation for women to plug into. My team and I hosted regular online experiences for thousands of women around the world to envision a reality of prosperity, expansion, and ambition of their lives. My Dare to Prosper Challenge supported over five thousand women in fifty-plus countries. Was I scared at times? Fuck yes. Did I come home to my truth and lead anyway? You better believe it.

The invitation here is not to be perfect; it's not even to be devoid of fear. The invitation now is to be aware of your use of language. Have fun with this practice and be patient as you're gaining awareness. See yourself as a leader, and recognize that in every conversation you're leading yourself and others either to fear or to love. In your family, with your friends, in your career, you are leading through your voice and language. What story about your life do you believe and are you passing on to others?

Our ancestors have handed down an inexhaustible supply of words, and we continue to develop them and create more every day. We get to choose how we use them. We can be grateful that we have the ability to describe our thoughts and feelings with ease and accuracy. Use your words with joy. Use your voice with reverence.

ASK YOURSELF

What words are you using? When you are talking to yourself, thinking, speaking to others, even writing, ask yourself:

- Does what I'm saying feel empowering?
- Does it make me feel light and expansive? Or is it heavy and contracting?
- Does it turn me on or off?

As you practice using language consciously and purposefully, you will see your life being created before your eyes. You will become lighter and happier purely because of how you use your language.

Sister, you have intuitive superpowers inside you that are just waiting for you to claim them — yes, you! You have the ability to speak ideas into existence through language. Dream big, love! The ideas inside you deserve to be brought into reality. Remember, this human experience can be entirely your creation if you choose.

Now that you have an expanded awareness of your words, I want to take you one cut deeper, into examining your thoughts. In the next chapter, we will take a fascinating look at the way your thoughts create your reality and learn how to activate the great law of attraction.

CHAPTER SIX

I Am What I Think

used to think that this world was a very scary and unsafe place. I used to think that things just happened at random — I could randomly get hurt, or someone could randomly steal something from me.

I gained a lot of inner peace and self-empowerment by understanding the law of attraction. The law of attraction reminds us that nothing can come into our experience without our being a vibrational match to it. Let me explain what I mean by "vibrational match."

You see, a lot exists all around us that we don't see with our eyes: energy, light waves, and sound vibrations. This is how Esther and Jerry Hicks, pioneering authors and teachers of the law of attraction, describe that phenomenon in their book *Manifest Your Desires*:

> You might see the powerful Law of Attraction as a sort of Universal Manager that sees to it that all thoughts that match one another line up. You understand this

principle when you turn on your radio and deliberately tune your receiver to match a signal from a broadcasting tower. You do not expect to hear music that is being broadcast on the radio frequency of 101 FM to be received on your tuner when it is set at 98.6 FM. You understand that radio vibrational frequencies must match, and the Law of Attraction agrees with you. Whatever you are giving your attention to causes you to emit a vibrational frequency and the vibrations that you offer equal your asking, which equals your point of attraction.

Basically, the law of attraction says that our thoughts create our reality. Everything we want to create, we have to think about first. When you expect something bad to happen, you are giving that thought energy, and your radio antenna is emitting its energetic frequency. As a result, the bad thing happens, and your thought about it becomes a self-fulfilling prophecy. Same thing goes with good things. I've attracted more blessings in my life than I could possibly count by focusing on them and visualizing them.

It's a bit like getting a college degree. You don't just create a college degree out of thin air. You decide what college you're going to go to, choose which classes you're going to take, and then from there you have the college experience. What happens in college is dependent on what you *think* about doing there, and then doing it. The same is true in the rest of life: to lead a purposeful life is to be intentional about what you're calling in.

We have a surprising level of control over what comes into our experience. All we need to do is understand ourselves as human radios, constantly emitting and receiving signals, and then intentionally tune ourselves to the signals matching what we desire — the fun and wonderful things we want to call into our lives.

It's the difference between living a conscious, created life or living on autopilot and accepting whatever may come your way. When you're living that way, letting things come to you at random, then you're not really *living* your life. You haven't fully accessed the superpowers of the creatrix within you. You're just playing the cards that get handed to you. Activating the law of attraction gets you out of autopilot and into empowerment and freedom. It reminds you that you are the ultimate creatrix of your experience. *You* get to call the shots; *you* get to say how it goes, as a co-creator alongside the universal, divine order.

Some of you may be thinking, "Wow, Jolie, that's really scary! Now I have to monitor my thoughts and be constantly worried about what I'm thinking!"

Not quite, sister. I invite you not to get caught in that headspace. While it can be a little scary at first, this is all just a practice, and you will master it soon! I remember when I first started working intentionally with my thoughts and I felt like, "Oh my gosh, am I thinking the right thing? Am I calling in what I want to call in?" Now I don't worry about it at all. You'll be fine. Promise.

So let's start by simply becoming aware of our thoughts.

Ask, Believe, Receive

Say you wake up, and it's raining outside. You might think, "Ugh, it's raining. I'm going to get wet, and I hate that. I hate when it rains. Something bad always happens when it rains." With those thoughts, you've just created an unconscious vibrational intention for "bad" things to happen.

Or you could look outside and say, "Yay, wow, it's raining. I'm so happy the trees are getting water and everything is going to be greener. I love snuggling up with a book on rainy days. I wonder how much comfort and coziness I can create today?" Do you see and feel the difference? Imagine what kind of day you'll have with those thoughts instead.

Another point to the law of attraction is that whatever you resist persists. That means that by focusing strongly on what you don't want, you actually call more of it in. Have you had a friend who was like, "I don't want to go out tonight, because if I do, I'm going to be bothered and want to leave," and then of course they do have a hard time with the night? They created an expectation of a bothered experience, and then it ended up happening.

Take a moment to check in with yourself. What are you resisting? Maybe you are resisting gaining weight. Maybe you're resisting communicating directly with a coworker. Maybe you're resisting being in a healthy relationship. Whatever it is, you keep bumping into it — probably because you're resisting it so hard!

What if you could release resistance? I know that may feel like a tall order, maybe not fully accessible, even. But what if you could just start with curiosity about a different possibility than the dread you've predicted? Could you be willing to envision an outcome that's light, easy, or joyous? That's the place to look, and it takes a bit of courage — and I already know you've got a massive reservoir of courage inside you, waiting to be tapped.

The law of attraction actually has three core components: (1) ask, (2) believe, and (3) receive. Let's look at each of these in turn.

1. Ask

The first step is the easiest. Think of the thing you want and ask life / the universe / God / yourself for it. When I started to get exceptionally clear in asking for what I wanted, my whole world expanded. I realized that I could have anything I put my mind to. This was really fun to play with. My creatrix turned on, and things started manifesting quickly around me.

ASK YOURSELF

What do you want? What could you start asking for? Ask yourself:

- Do I desire to experience more prosperity?
- Do I want a contributive, harmonious romantic partnership?
- Do I want to start a family?
- Do I want more ease and love with my family?
- Do I want a better place to live and more inspiring surroundings?
- Do I want more professional success?
- Do I want more creativity?
- Do I want to experience more health and vitality?
- Do I want to have a more open heart?
- Do I wish to access more of my courage?

Ask for these things. Believe that you're worthy of having it all, because you were born worthy. Whatever you want in your life, the key to getting it is being courageous enough to ask for it.

2. Believe

The second step, to believe you deserve to have it, is a little harder. For many people who read Rhonda Byrne's book *The Secret* (probably the most famous book about the law of attraction) or saw the film it was based on, this step was where the process fell apart: they didn't believe they were worthy to receive the things they asked for.

We are so good at judging ourselves for not being worthy to have the things we say we want. For example, you might say, "I want that million-dollar mansion over there," but at the same time you're judging people for being rich or judging yourself for not working hard enough. Deep down, you may not actually believe that you deserve that beautiful house. And if you don't believe you're worthy, you'll likely never call it into your experience.

You say you want more money, but you don't think you're responsible enough to manage money. You say you want the relationship, but you don't trust yourself because of how your relationships turned out in the past. In order to have that which you're asking for, you have to believe you are deserving of it. I'm going to say that one more time: *You have to believe it.*

You may be asking, "Well, how do I believe it? I don't know how to change my beliefs!"

Start with something small. One of my favorite ways to practice is to accept a compliment. How often do we deflect compliments? Someone says, "Hey, nice shirt," and we respond, "This thing? It's not special at all." Or we just say, "Oh no, I like *your* shirt!" If you want to start strengthening your belief muscle, when someone gives you a compliment, allow yourself to take it in. Believing yourself smart or beautiful or accomplished enough to accept a compliment is a great start to feeling worthy, girlfriend.

Another way is to bring this practice to your journal. Write out the story of your life unfolding according to your highest desires, and envision yourself receiving it, one small step at a time. If you try to take a giant leap, like going from having $0 to your name to manifesting $1 million, it's likely too big of a leap for you to actually believe in and get on board with. Starting small may sound like this: "Today I'm feeling anxious about money. I'm going to honor that there is fear inside me and not make myself wrong for feeling it. In this moment, I choose to see how truly abundant my life is. I have a safe home, loving friends, and food to eat. Today I will nourish myself and be gentle with the parts of me that feel afraid. I can see my life already changing for the better. I believe in myself to see opportunities for my life, to reach out for support, to fill up on the self-love I have been seeking in others. I believe my prosperity is unfolding right before my eyes. I believe in my dream to buy a home. I believe in better days ahead."

Just this simple act of loving self-talk and acknowledgment of your fears will help you tremendously in being able to believe that more is coming for you.

3. Receive

Oh my gosh, do we women have a hard time with step 3, receiving! To be able to receive, you have to be willing to actually *have* the thing you say you want. So many people I know say that they want to make $10,000 a month, for example, but in reality, they're not willing to receive it.

What do I mean by that? It comes back to the worthiness conversation. If you don't really believe you are worthy of $10,000 a month (or $20,000, or $50,000), or if you have conflicting beliefs running in the background (such as "I want it but I also believe that it's not safe to have it"), then you won't be able to receive it. To receive something is to actually take it on, and that means assuming responsibility. There's a lot we *could* receive but we just *don't* because on some level we don't want the responsibility.

How often do people want to give us things, and we turn them down, we just say no? In the early days of my business, a friend offered to make me a website as a gift when I really needed a website. They had the resources to support me, they believed in my mission, and they said it was a joy for them to help. My mind made up all these reasons why I couldn't receive their offer! I didn't want to accept charity, I wanted to do it myself, I'd have to figure out what I wanted for my website, I didn't have money to pay them, and on and on. But then I thought, "No. This would be such a contribution to me. And I will pay it forward. I will receive this." In the end I had a beautiful experience of receiving.

Eventually I got into the practice of saying, "Received." Going back to the example of compliments, when somebody would say, "I really like your hair today!" I would respond, "Thank you, received." I also found, in giving compliments, that it feels so good to be received by others. Give people the gift of receiving their compliments. Use the actual word, and feel the magic happening.

Activating the Law of Attraction

If you want to take on the law of attraction, you have to master these three components: to ask, to believe that you're worthy of receiving what you asked for, and then to actually allow yourself to receive it.

Activating the law of attraction in your life is a huge step toward being truly empowered. Now I want to give you some examples of how you can start activating it.

- ASK YOURSELF QUESTIONS. Something I have learned to ask myself is "How does it get better?" Asking this question shows that you are willing to have more. You are literally casting out a request to the universe, a request to God, to discover what else is possible.

   I also start a lot of questions with "I wonder..." — for example, "I wonder what it would take to feel like a million bucks today? I wonder what it would take to make $10,000 this month? I wonder what it would be like to just be in my body and have fun when I go out dancing tonight?" Get into the habit of asking yourself questions. You can do this in your journal; you can do it in your mind; you can even do it out loud.

- EXPRESS GRATITUDE. Another practice that I like to use to activate the law of attraction is the art of gratitude. Remember how one of the ways to journal is to express gratitude? Years ago, I got into the habit of beginning every morning by saying five things that I'm grateful for. Sometimes they're very simple things: "I'm grateful that my legs work. I'm grateful to be in perfect health. I'm grateful that I can see. I'm grateful for running water. I'm grateful that I can hear music." Your journal is the perfect place to keep a consistent log of your gratitude and appreciation for your life.

   The more you do this, the more you will attract

good things into your life. I recommend using your new journal practice to constantly remind yourself what you're grateful for, because it's far too easy to dwell in the negative. Our primal brains are wired for survival and have the tendency to overdo the worse-case scenario. And remember, when you dwell in the negative and ask questions like "How much worse can this get?" the universe will show you how it gets worse.

- **VISUALIZE.** My last activation tool is visualization. I use my journal for this as well. I write out where I'll be in one year from now, as if I'm already there: "I'm being the contribution in the world that I know I can be. I'm speaking on sold-out stages. I'm impacting millions of people's lives. I'm a *New York Times* bestselling author. I'm having so much fun with my life. I am a seven-figure earner while traveling the world and living in my joy." When you call in what you'll have in the future, you get to experience the excitement of having it *right now*. Get in the practice of visualizing where you're going, and you'll be able to call in your life's path with so much ease.

Receiving True Prosperity

I'll be honest with you: the first thing many people think of when they hear about the law of attraction is money. Call it "prosperity," call it "abundance," call it "resources," but whatever you call it, not having it is one of the major stressors people experience in this world. Most of us dream about the freedom we would get from having more of it or at least from never worrying about having enough. With that truth in mind, and since this is one of my specialty areas in the seminars and courses I teach, let's talk about the law of attraction in terms of the fascinating, complex, seductive, elusive energy we call money.

The law of attraction is powerful when it comes to your prosperity work, because the outer world ends up mirroring what you feel on the inside. But, as with anything you want to manifest, creating prosperity is about more than thought. It's about action.

For many people, energetic blockages around money began in childhood. This was the case for me. I remember the day my mom's car was repossessed and I had to walk to school. Because I grew up with two parents who struggled with gambling and scarcity mentality, money is often a big issue. Addiction is a bottomless pit; money falls into it, never to be seen again. And many times throughout my adult life, when I have felt emotionally stuck, money was involved. It takes awareness and effort to break the cycle of a thinking process that has become unconscious but is blocking your flow of money energy.

Here are a few ways I've learned to begin dissolving those blockages.

- DISRUPT YOUR ROUTINE. We need to step out of our routines so we can look at our lives. Through contemplation and self-reflection, we can become more aware of the unconscious scripts we have playing in the background. For example, I'm no longer a child living in a household with addiction energy, but when I'm not conscious and fall into a routine, I can default to the old fear and scarcity of my childhood.

- **OBSERVE YOUR THOUGHTS.** All of us possess a level of self-awareness *beyond* thought that can *observe* thought. Try observing your thoughts without responding to them so that they no longer initiate the automatic biochemical responses that produce habitual behavior. Step back and see the automatic program that's running. You might have a disempowering thought about money and then observe: "Okay, that's interesting. As soon as I look at my money, I feel this deep sense of guilt and fear." Or you might notice, "As soon as I look at my future, and my retirement plan, and my wealth, I am overwhelmed by this crushing sensation of fear that I haven't done enough." To separate action from the programmed thought process allows us to have dominion over the thought process, which disempowers it.

- **BE AWARE OF YOUR ACTIONS.** Ultimately, we can exercise control over what we do in response to our thoughts. This disconnects the behaviors that have become hardwired into our brains. It's not your fault that you repeat patterns of scarcity, but you do have the power to break the patterns by practicing thought awareness.

No matter what you've been through in your life, no matter how deep you think your wounds are around money, no matter how many times you feel like you've fallen on your ass with money, no matter how much you've been judging yourself lately about repeating the past or not owning your worth or being afraid of charging high-end prices in business (this is very common for women and also for creatives), there's always,

always a new way to rewire your brain and create a new relationship with your prosperity.

What Is Money?

When systems are built before we come into the picture — like the programming already in place in our childhood homes — we tend to accept the reality we're exposed to instead of questioning it. Money has always been a part of our lives, and we are all programmed to see it and understand it and react to it according to our experiences. The result is that we have all developed our own unique relationship with money, in many cases never taking a step back to consciously look at that relationship and question it: "Is my inherited relationship with money the relationship that I'm committed to? Or is there something else here that I would like to develop?"

Let's take a look at what money actually is. It's not just pieces of paper, and it's not just numbers in your bank account. It's so much more. I see money as a choice multiplier. To have money means that you have more choices in your life. "I want to go where I want to go when I want to go there. I want to be able to travel. I want to be able to buy my friends awesome gifts. I want to be able to invest in my business and get my work out there." You don't have to deny yourself anything when you have sufficient money.

Money also reflects your gratitude and attitude around service. If you are somebody who wakes up in the morning with the mantras "Whom can I serve today? How can I create love today? Whom can I love today?" and you are making an impact with your love, inevitably money follows that.

However, there's a shadow side to this principle of

generosity. The over-givers and the people pleasers reverse that flow when they neglect to ask for their money. Remember that you also have to be willing to receive. Money is, along with all the other things I've mentioned, a measure of your willingness and capacity to receive.

Too, money carries with it the illusion that it is a panacea. We've all heard the stories about the billionaires who feel empty inside, and we may scoff at them and think, "If *I* were rich, I'd be completely happy." But the truth is that happiness doesn't have anything to do with money. Money's not going to solve your problem with not feeling good. Choice, freedom, opportunity, and ease can all be influenced by money, but real happiness comes only when you are deeply fulfilled in your spiritual practice and you are on your path of destiny. If you also have money, then that's a fucking good life. You *deserve* a life like that! (But remember, you have to *believe* you deserve it!)

It's a process, but you can work on being here right now with your prosperity, my love. Be here right now. Choose it right now. Don't project that maybe you'll get it sometime in the future. Don't believe you'll feel better when you have it. The practice of prosperity is finding ways to notice how you are prosperous right now. If the only thing that you have in your life is your breath, you can tap into your infinite prosperity by knowing that life has got you, with oxygen surrounding you in a limitless supply, and that you are always, always supported and taken care of. If you ever forget about your prosperity and you're feeling broke and the bills are crushing you and this whole system just feels scary, go out in nature and observe beauty. Take in the wealth all around you in a new way. Money is going to look for the people exuding the highest vibrational consciousness. It takes your intentional effort to create that consciousness.

A lot of billionaires know the game and play the system. This system is meant for you to play. It's built that way. It's built in such a way that a lot of people remain in the status quo of the bottom tier of poverty, then maybe there are some in the middle class, maybe some in the upper middle class. But to actually play outside of that paradigm, you have to become your own paradigm. I knew from a young age that I didn't want to play that game of "Gosh, I hope I hit these performance metrics so I can make a 10 percent raise every year." I wanted more. Ask yourself: Am I playing the game of money, *or is it playing me*?

The truth is that money is an imaginary system created in the minds of humans. No other species on the planet places value on anything resembling money. We created this game, so we can play with it and manipulate it in the same way that it was created — in our minds. To be played by money means that you feel crushed underneath it, like it's an external force outside you that will always threaten your freedom. Being played is that feeling that no matter how hard you try, you'll never get ahead. Have you felt that way before? How much do you feel that right now?

Money used to be backed by gold, a real, tangible earth element. It's not anymore. It's a digital number on digital screens. We all know the banks don't even have our money. If we all decided to withdraw our money from the banks, we would discover it isn't all there. It's an imaginary system based on a human agreement. But you can change the flow whenever you want to. You have to be willing to learn how to play the game of money.

When you use your power to be able to see your prosperity and feel it and believe it, you develop a frequency match with money. What continually blocks us from doing this? It's our belief system. Use the power of visualization to see it for your-self, to believe it for yourself, and to change and ripen your relationship with prosperity.

Your winning is the greatest gift you can give to the world, sweetheart — believe that. When you have resources, you can serve more people.

Right now, don't worry about the how. I invite you to con-nect to the feeling of having what you want and what you need and committing to becoming the creatrix of that vision.

Women, Money, and Skin Color

It wasn't until very recently in our Western timeline that it was socially acceptable for women to make money on their own, let alone be celebrated for it. As women, we're still healing the collective wound from the belief that "it's not a woman's place to create success or prosperity."

The Equal Credit Opportunity Act came along in 1974. It prohibited discrimination by any creditor based on sex, mari-tal status, religion, national origin, or age in connection to the approval or denial of credit. Prior to 1974, if you were a woman who wanted to open a credit card in your own name, you could easily have been told that you needed your husband's signa-ture. If you were Muslim, or Black, or Brown, or "too old," or simply didn't fit into the subjective, limited, White man's view of who was deemed to be "creditworthy," you could be denied with no other explanation. Fucked up, huh? The year 1974 was not that long ago, essentially just two generations back. Think about that. We women still feel the lingering effects of that dis-crimination.

If you're a woman of color, a Black or Brown woman in the United States specifically, your inherited money reality was likely much different from that of a White woman. As a White woman myself, I am aware of the privilege that has come with my skin color. I will never pretend that my own trauma around money is even remotely similar to the trauma that a Black or Brown woman may have endured, and that many continue to endure. Many women of color that I know have had family trauma with money that was more severe than my own, on top of the oppressive, racist limits placed on them in other areas of life.

Another example of justice coming way too late was the landmark 1968 US Supreme Court case *Jones v. Alfred H. Mayer Co.* This decision finally made it possible for Congress to prohibit racial discrimination in the sale of a property. For over a century, many Black people in America had not been able to invest in real estate and land. They were blatantly denied, shunned, and forced out of neighborhoods. The reality was very different for White people, who were often able to build generational wealth through real estate. The lingering wounds for people of color are real, the trauma of slavery is undeniable, and the effects are very much alive in the present day.

As a woman who leads other women, it's important for me to be humble in knowing that just because I'm a woman like you, I don't know your exact circumstances or your unique pain concerning money. But what I do know for certain is that fear created these divisions, and love is the only way to eliminate them. I'm still learning, and I'm committed to being a lifelong student of how I can truly be an ally and an accomplice for my Black and Brown sisters.

If you are a woman of color, I have a special conversation just for you at joliedawn.com/esf. It would be an honor if you joined us.

We all have our unique wounds, inherited beliefs, and neuroses concerning money. What has been your experience? How has your skin color — White, Brown, Black, or any shade in between — played a role? How did your family ethnicity or ethnicities play a role in your generational relationship with money? Take a moment to reflect. This is a perfect journaling moment.

Scarcity versus Abundance

Let's take a look at one of the primary blockages to experiencing true and lasting prosperity for all humans: a repetitive story of poverty and scarcity that we replay in our heads, versus one of abundance and prosperity. Most of us know what scarcity feels like, and most of us also know the good, spacious feeling of having enough (even if it's only been for brief moments).

The trick is not to allow habits to get us stuck in scarcity. We compare ourselves to others; we judge other people for having money; we get stuck in dark loops and don't know how to get out. Think back to chapter 5, where we discussed the power of language. We stay stuck when we use scarcity language: "I want that, but I can't have it. I can't go there. I can't do that. I can't learn that. I can't be that." If we habitually deny ourselves experiences because we automatically assume we don't have money for them, we live a life of being played by money. Money does not deserve to have that much power over you and your life enjoyment. Can we agree on that?

Now before you say, "But Jolie! It's not just a 'story' of scarcity. It's real for me. The rent is due, and I am stressed. I can't just 'mindset' my way to prosperity around this." Girl, I get it. I really do know what it's like to feel the crippling fear of not being able to pay bills and the gut-wrenching sadness of having to deny yourself the things you desire. Let me tell you, more scarcity and fear is not the path to the freedom you desire. When scarcity increases, it's very challenging to think creatively for solutions. My invitation here is to bring awareness to automatic behaviors and responses. To breathe a moment of space between stimulus and response, between opening an unexpected bill and feeling panic. The secret of true prosperity is being able to generate it as a *feeling* even before you can manifest it as a physical reality. I know this practice can feel hard. But you are so much more powerful and capable than you give yourself credit for.

Maybe for you, it's not an issue of generating enough money to pay your bills. Maybe you've found your path of a lucrative life and/or ample support from others. Maybe the next-level prosperity upgrade is to relax in your body, trust your money, give yourself the freedom to spend money on yourself. Or, on the opposite side of the spectrum, maybe your challenge is to love yourself enough to save for the future. No matter where you are right now, the way out is to become more aware of the repetitive story in your head around scarcity and to consciously choose a narrative of prosperity.

So many women I've worked with over the years have a story around their age. "I'm thirty. I should have _____ by now." Or, "I'm forty. I should have had this." Whether we're twenty-five, or sixty, or seventy, or eighty, this idea in our heads of what we thought each age was going to be like often revolves around money.

Begin noticing your language around money. Do you say things like these? "Real estate is so expensive these days!" "I could never afford a nice car!" "I wish I could wear things like that." "I'll never be able to make my rent this month!" "I can't pay these bills! Life is so expensive!" Think about what you call in when you say or even think these things.

Then there is the heavy, burdensome subject of debt. Many people can't bear to look closely at their debt because it's too terrifying. I remember being like that — not wanting to know my credit card balances, feeling guilty about owing money, believing I had the poverty gene and couldn't do anything about it, thinking nothing would ever change and it was just who I was, who I would always be, who my family had always been.

None of that is true. None of it! There's always a new future and a different path available to you, if you choose.

Any thought, sensation, or emotion that makes you feel bad, contracted, or heavy when you think about money is keeping you stuck. Look back through your life. Ask yourself when you started feeling this way about money. What belief about money that's no longer serving you are you ready to release? It might be something that helped you survive at some point, but you don't need it anymore. It's time to modernize, to clean up your thoughts, and to look with clear eyes at what is actually available to you — which is everything.

Shame and guilt are among the lowest vibrational frequencies in the human experience, right above death. If we think of death as a flat line, shame and guilt are low, slow, barely discernible vibrations. It's not about good and bad. It's about what makes you vibrate high and what makes you vibrate low. Shame and guilt make you feel bad about yourself, that you're inherently wrong as a person. They keep you locked into scarcity. If you aren't enough, then how can you ever have enough?

Of course, the systems in place are meant to keep you in debt, forever compounding interest and compounding shame. Plenty of people profit from the debt-shame paradigm. If you're in debt, big or small, have you ever asked yourself how it happened? Look at student loans. It's fucking crazy what kind of interest rates institutions get for student loans. I see my friends feeling crushed under student loan debt and filled with shame and guilt. They think they did this to themselves and they are bad, but the truth is that it's not entirely their fault.

Our monetary system has a history of preying upon vulnerable people. Look what happened in 2008: people were given mortgages that they weren't qualified for, until the whole house of cards collapsed. It takes conscious effort to say, "I'm not going to get stuck in feeling guilt and shame about this. I trust that I am where I need to be right now. I trust in my ability to creatively problem-solve and find a way out."

Another low-vibrational feeling is jealousy, which is believing you can't have what somebody else has. Jealousy has an obsessive, hoarding energy around it. Yet another one is doubt, when you believe that something isn't even possible for you. Insecurity means you feel like you are on shaky ground. Anxiety and fear, denial and anger — they all influence the flow of energy toward or away from you.

Instead of saying things like "I want that, but I can't have it," think, "I could totally have it. I don't choose it right now, but I can choose it whenever I want to." This is you taking back your choice.

Celebrating Money

One of the most powerful things I did in my money journey was celebrate every single dollar that came onto my path. I counted it, rejoiced in it, worshipped it as if it were holy, because it is. This attitude is what makes money *want* to come to you! Money loves to be appreciated.

I enjoy always having cash around me. In my wallet, in my car, in random drawers, in my safe, on my altar. I love it. I love being with it. I love smelling it. I bring it on my retreats, and I perform healing rituals with it. It fills me with gratitude. I love it so much because its tangibleness reminds me of what I actually have. In this digital world, we can be disconnected from what money is, which is why I love physical money. I revel in it.

One of my rituals has been to put up a big dry-erase whiteboard that has a whole year's calendar with little circles or squares for each day. Every time I get paid, I write it on the calendar. I've been doing this for five years. I can see what I earn. I can count it. I value it. I get excited about it. Being able to see the numbers without having to look back at my bank statement makes the money feel special, energetic, exciting. It helps me feel the receiving of it.

If you're an entrepreneur, know exactly what tasks in your business make you the most money. Keep those activities close; keep them sacred. Know the fruits of your labor. Energetically speaking, money is a living, breathing entity that comes in abundance, and then leaves, and comes, and then leaves. If you're riding an emotional roller coaster and tying your worth to money, you're setting yourself up to fail. It took me years to fully understand this. Get to know money. Spend time with it. Watch it, measure it, grow it. In short, allow money to make you feel good, honey. Let money make you feel sweet in your body.

The universe responds to what you're projecting, so project abundance: "Oh, yes. Abundance, yes. I just got paid. This feels so good. I'm going to celebrate that." If you're just like, "Oh my God! It was only this much money. Why wasn't it more?" then there goes the energy away from you again.

If your record has been playing a song of insecurity, doubt, and shame, we need to find a new song for you. Write letters to money (see the journaling exercise later in this chapter). Pay attention to money. Love money. It's not wrong. It's not selfish or greedy. It's romantic and beautiful.

Wealth is a mindset. Affluence is a mindset. It's a feeling that you practice. It's the way that you envision your future. There's no story or money history that can't be turned around, yes, even yours.

Attracting Money Miracles

When I created the first Dare to Prosper Challenge in 2019, I set out with an experiment: How could I create a tangible impact on women's money reality using energy healing and mindset tools? The result was a live, daily visualization experience, open to anyone who identified as a woman, no matter their culture, background, or spiritual beliefs. I focused on working with women because the feminine experience is unique and it allows me to facilitate a specialized conversation. I combined many tools and modalities that I had studied over the years: unconscious reprogramming, hypnosis, kundalini yoga and breath work, visualization, and theta healing. I guided thousands of women every morning to get quiet and go inward to experience a profound healing in their relationship with money. I used the metaphor of a "prosperity garden," and every day we came to the garden to pull the weeds and plant seeds for the future.

It blew my mind to witness all the miracles we created in ten days. I wept happy tears as the testimonials poured in: women getting unexpected raises, finding thousands of dollars that they had forgotten about, raising their rates and signing clients, having huge breakthroughs in their relationships, feeling more lightness and ease, and on and on. One woman even got a surprise check for $300,000! It was nothing short of miraculous, and the creative power was palpable.

If you're curious to experience the Dare to Prosper Challenge, head to joliedawn.com/esf, and you can take the ten-day journey for yourself.

Prosperity is an inside job, and true wealth is created first as energy, through our thoughts. We can use the law of attraction to expand on what we believe is possible for us.

It really isn't as complex as we make it out to be. It's just a matter of being consciously aware of your thoughts. The lighter your thoughts are, the more lightness you'll call in. The darker your thoughts are, the more darkness you'll call in. To be aware of the lightness, stay in the space of gratitude, visualize what you want, and be the commander of your own experience. Ask, believe, and receive. You can do this. You already are, right now.

If you're open, and if you're focused on expansion, possibility, and your own vibration, miracles are a natural occurrence, and you can call more of them into your life. You deserve abundance, freedom, and pleasure. You deserve a life built entirely of your creation. Are you willing to own that?

I dare you to break societal norms and cultural conditioning, to put logic and "realistic thinking" aside, to stop believing the lie of scarcity to recommit to your natural state of prosperity.

Wealth Consciousness as a Spiritual Practice

Improving your money relationship starts with you committing to a daily practice. I say "practice" because I mean that: it's an ever-changing energetic relationship that requires consistent awareness. It requires devotion. Every day, devote time to upgrading your money mindset. This practice can consist of meditation, visualization, or journaling. The four-part journaling exercise below is a great place to start.

MONEY JOURNALING EXERCISE

Pull out your journal, get quiet, and spend some time reflecting on the prompts below.

1. Letter to Money

Write a letter to money, declaring a new relationship with it as you would to a distant lover. What would you like to say? How do you propose you will change things? What are you now aware of that you weren't before?

2. Letter from Money to You

Write a letter from money to you. What does money want to say? Does money want to be with you? How would money like your relationship to be different?

3. Mom's / Dad's / Caretaker's Money Habits, Stories, and Judgments

Write down the main beliefs about money held by each adult that raised you. After you write out the extensive list, circle the beliefs that you inherited or may be playing out. If this exercise brings up a lot of emotions, feel the feelings, breathe through the memories, and seek support from a friend or therapist if you need it.

4. *Your Money Relationship*

Answer the following questions:

- What is your current relationship to money?
- How do you feel when you think about money?
- What conversations do you currently have around money?
- What new future are you committed to creating with money?

It takes a bold woman to own her desires, to unapologetically want what she wants, to live outside the noise of shame, guilt, doubt, and fear. Bring your love to your money and shine the light on everyone around you. The world heals when we all rise into prosperity. The world heals when the systems start working for everyone.

Dare to let go of your pain, the past version of you, distrust, and resignation.

Dare to set up your future with bold audacity to own your highest worth.

Dare to thrive, even in an uncertain economy.

Dare to be a prosperity rebel, a fringe optimist.

Dare to be the *you* that you came here to be, before anyone made you believe in anything other than magic.

Dare to be the creatrix of your life.

CHAPTER SEVEN

I Reclaim My Sexual

Innocence

So, woman, you say you want to be sexy? Well, in the last chapter you learned that you are what you think. It follows that being sexy starts with you believing that you're sexy, feeling that you're sexy, embodying the knowing that you're sexy. Our sexuality is truly the epicenter of our manifestation power as women. Feminine power relies on us being sexually healed and expressed. I struggled with this for years, and many of my clients have as well. In this chapter, you will learn what distinguishes a sexually vibrant woman who stands in her creative powers from all the rest.

I'm going to be real with you here. It took a whole new level of bravery for me to put this story out to you. For so long, my sexuality was a deep root of pain and shame, confusion and wrongness and embarrassment. I did not think I was beautiful. I did not think I was worthy. I did not think I was desirable. The shame that I had in my body around my sexuality, around sex, around my sexual history, was *crushing*. This was the result of trauma stored in my body — years of judgment and disgust that I had for myself.

Over time, I made a full 180-degree turn from those feelings. With lots of healing work and help from highly trained coaches, I am happy to say that today I truly love being in my body and I feel integrated with my sexual past. I've worked hard to reclaim my sexual innocence. And yet, even with hundreds of hours of healing work behind me, writing about my past was incredibly confronting.

I bet some of you can relate. Maybe you've been through a similar journey to loving yourself and owning your sexuality. Maybe you're partway into yours. Maybe you're just starting.

The good news is, it doesn't matter where you are on that journey. Wherever you are right now is perfect, because it's where you are. In this chapter, I want to help you move a few more steps in a self-affirming direction. When we're finished, you'll be that much closer to seeing your unique beauty and owning yourself as a sexually vibrant, fully embodied woman.

"What difference would that actually make in my life?" you might be asking. Are you ready?

I imagine some of you started out much like I did, whether you had a family like mine or just picked up the collective pain and suppression around sexuality in our culture. I grew up in a Christian household where sex was seen as the ultimate sin. My parents reinforced this repeatedly in my upbringing, vocally judging people who had sex before marriage, often commenting on female celebrities who were "sluts" because they were sleeping with their boyfriends. So I grew up thinking that sex was wrong, bad, something to be judged and shamed for doing. Definitely not something to be free and self-expressed around.

But at the same time, I was celebrated for being sexy. I bought sexy clothes, I listened to Britney Spears, I had full cleavage really young, and I often wore revealing outfits to school. People noticed me, and I liked being admired... yet in my mind, deep down, my sexuality was still wrong. Sexy was good, but sexual was bad. It was confusing, to say the least.

And, worse, I had no tools to deal with my own sexuality. I always felt super weird and off, like, "Why do I have so much sexual energy, and why do I want to explore? If this is wrong, why do I want to do it so much?" And when someone tells you that you can't do something or that it's wrong, suddenly a whole new desire kicks in to do the forbidden thing! That's what happened to me. What my parents thought would be saving me from heartache actually created years of it, because it doesn't work to say sex is bad without providing any tools or perspective on how to approach sex consciously or view it as a sacred act. All I had was my own simmering sexual energy and the mandate: "Just don't do it."

So I did everything but.

At age eleven, I started exploring, and by fourteen, getting to "third base" was common. I justified it as, "Well, it wasn't sex." When I started feeling embarrassed seeing boys in school I'd gotten to third base with over the weekend, I solved that problem by going for older boys — boys outside of my school.

Alcohol helped. I was a completely different person when I was drinking. I was sexually vibrant. I would kiss any guy. I felt desired. I felt wanted. I felt funny and vivacious and attractive. It was only when I sobered up that I felt the rush of shame and embarrassment.

For many years, my sexual exploration happened only when I was under the influence and usually with people I didn't even like. Because I thought sex was so wrong, I would allow it when I was already being really bad and wrong anyway, like when I was blackout drunk or not fully aware of what I was doing. That was how I justified it: "I don't remember it, so it didn't really happen." (Weirdly, the girls who had consistent boyfriends and had healthy sex lives I deemed "sluts," because they were doing it consciously! That shows how skewed my ideas of sex were at that time.)

I didn't have sober sex until I was twenty-two and had been with my boyfriend for a year. *One entire year.* For the first year of us dating, every time we were going to be sexually intimate, I would down shots. I thought this was normal at the time — take a couple shots of tequila, loosen up. But I realized I was just numbing myself out because I couldn't face my sexuality being sober. I didn't know how.

For years after that, I didn't think I could talk about it. I believed that if I mentioned my sexual past, no guy would want me. If I acknowledged my years of drunken sex, I would come off as weak and irresponsible or else be tarred with the same brush my parents used on sexually active celebrities. And if I talked about it even to myself, I'd have to face the fact that I let a lot of people take my innocence from me. If I had been sober, in a lot of those sexual situations I'd have said, "No." But because I was always drunk and not fully aware of what was happening, I let a lot of (what should have been) nonconsensual sex happen to me. I let my body be misused because I was too drunk to care. For a long time, I just couldn't face that.

But eventually, I realized that shame only lives in darkness. It only lives when it's in the dark corners of your memory, where no one sees it but you. When you talk about something and when you're willing to shed the light on it, the shame loosens its grip. When you allow the light in, you create a space of healing.

Dealing with Guilt, Shame...and God

A big part of my healing was coming to terms with my religious upbringing. Even in my most desperate, dark times, I believed in God, but I always felt like God was mad at me for being inherently rebellious and inherently sexual. I felt so judged: my sexuality was wrong, and I shouldn't want to be with boys, I shouldn't want to be sexual, I shouldn't want to drink. But I wanted all those things, so I wondered, "What is wrong with me for having these desires? What is wrong with me for wanting to explore sex so much?" There was this shame and toxic weight in my body, and I was so quick to make myself wrong because if God thought I was wrong, it must be true. I didn't feel beautiful; I thought that God hated me. I thought I was totally forsaken.

This was so painful that eventually I just said, "Screw spirituality" and left my religion entirely. For the next several years, I didn't pray, I stayed away from church, and I didn't even use the word *God* in my vocabulary. That was an incredibly lonely and disconnected time for me. I completely forgot who I was. I felt trapped in the day-to-day struggle of life. I filled my time with drinking, partying, and every other distraction I could find. I felt very alone and afraid. The only place I knew that might inspire me again was a church environment, but church was the place where I'd felt the most judged and compared and sized up. I couldn't and wouldn't go back there. They didn't want someone like me. So I remained spiritually disconnected.

Some of you may also have dealt with feelings of shame

and wrongness from your childhood religion. Maybe you had a similar experience in your religion, but even if you did not grow up in a religious family, these dogmas are written into the DNA of our culture, so you may have encountered the same kind of judgment anyway.

So how did I — and how do you — get past all that shit and find your actual connection with God? And perhaps more importantly, given all the feelings of shame and wrongness we just talked about, why would you want to?

For me, it started when I read the book *Conversations with God* by Neale Donald Walsch. All I can say is, "Just wow." If you haven't read it, I really recommend it. The book is based on a statement that sages have been making for centuries: "God is within you. You and God are inseparable." When I read that, it was like a lightning bolt: God never judged me! I was never wrong. The separation I'd felt from God for so many years didn't even exist. I was floored — and flooded with hope for the first time in years.

As I kept reading, I began to understand that heaven is a state of mind, a state of being. True empowerment doesn't come from believing in some blissful afterlife you'll see if you've been a good little girl but, rather, from giving yourself permission to reach within and experience that bliss now, while you're in your human body. You can release yourself from making yourself wrong, and you can give yourself a break from unconscious self-shaming. There are reservoirs of bliss inside you that you haven't tapped yet — I believe this is what Jesus meant when he said things like "The kingdom of heaven is within you." As I started to let go of my judgments and preconceived notions of what I thought God was, I started to tap into that bliss inside myself.

As I began to heal, I sought out people to talk to who would hold a space of nonjudgment for me — people who could accept me for me and not judge me for what had happened in the past. One of the most healing things anyone has ever said to me was when my boyfriend told me, early in our relationship, "I don't believe in any such thing as a 'slut.'" I had never before heard anyone be so open and accepting in my life.

As I share my past with you now, I no longer feel shame or wrongness around it. It just is what it is. It's a piece of my past; it doesn't make me who I am. It's just something that I experienced and learned a lot from. By shining light on the shame and sharing about it with you, I'm taking steps to release and remove it entirely.

Bringing Shadow Sexuality into the Light

Our ticket into this human experience is our body. We've all been created as absolute masterpieces. If the most brilliant scientists, engineers, and geneticists tried to replicate the human body, it would be a multibillion-dollar feat, and yet the result wouldn't even come close to having the magical powers that a real human body possesses. And guess what? *You* are the owner of a human body. Every day, you get to play with the most awe-inspiring, mysterious creation that God made. The hand that created you is the hand that creates it all. You're pretty magnificent, eh?

So I want you to check in with yourself, sister. Do you have sexual shame from the past? Do you have any sexual trauma that you have been unwilling to talk about? What memories are sitting in the dark corners of your mind, dishonoring you for what is in reality the beauty of your sexuality?

It's all right if you do. Many women carry around shame regarding sexuality. We don't think it's safe to be a woman. Too many women have been molested, abused, raped, taken advantage of, and hurt. Centuries of sexual repression, sexual control, sexual torture in wartime, and sexual abuse in peacetime live in the collective memory of all women. A woman's sexuality is fundamental to her power. If you want to control a woman, control her sexuality. It's a very effective strategy. Today, we have the right to declare the end of others controlling our sex and sexuality. It's our body. Our choice. Our life-force energy.

Way too much abuse is still happening to women today. We are still socialized and expected to give away our sexual power or allow it to be taken from us. Our sexuality is used to manipulate us, control us, limit us, and shame us. Even when these effects aren't intentional, we sometimes become our own victims by underestimating the emotional connections we form when we have sex.

Sometimes we even embrace the dark sides of our sexuality. For me this took the form of wild, semiconscious promiscuity. For some women, it's using sex to manipulate men — providing it as a reward, threatening their manhood with it, getting them to stay even when they don't want a relationship, or "accidentally" getting pregnant in order to feel safe. By doing these unworthy things, we undermine our own sexual power just as surely as if someone else were taking it away.

My road to healing my own sexual shame has been a long one, and dealing with it is still a constant practice. As I mentioned, it took a lot for me to even include it in this book. Healing has come about *because* I've been willing to talk about my darkness and bring it into the light. I'm not willing to have it be a secret anymore, because that is how it takes away my power.

I encourage you to look within yourself and find the dark

places where you've held on to sexual shame. Where you've allowed your sexual power to be taken from you. Where you've been hurt or manipulated or taken advantage of. And when you find those places, gently ask yourself what you need to do to bring them into the light.

Embracing Your Sexual Liberation

How do we even do that? For starters, let's redefine what sexuality means to us.

To me, sexuality means remembering how sacred my womb space actually is. Life is created here; all creativity is born here. Everything around that space, including the act that allows it to create life, is sacred and beautiful. A truly expressed woman is in touch with the reality of how beautiful her body is, how sacred her womb space is, how sacred her sexuality is. She knows that she is beautiful and worthy, and she trusts herself.

A sexually free woman has five distinct characteristics:

1. She loves her body.
2. She has healthy boundaries.
3. She honors her "no" with no need for explanation.
4. She faces her past and seeks healing.
5. She embodies her unique expression of sexy.

Let's look at each of these in detail so you can rock your version of empowered sexuality.

Loving Your Body

A free and sexual woman embraces all parts of herself. She is able to find beauty in her face, in her body, in her breasts, in her curves. She loves the way that she looks. She doesn't need external validation to know that she's beautiful. She honors her body with good food and exercise, and she treats her body like the temple it really is.

The way that you love yourself is going to be the basis for how anybody else can love you. That means the very basis for being a fully sexually expressed woman is being in love with yourself and your body. Nobody will ever love you as much as you love yourself.

I love to acknowledge all parts of my body, whether it's in a bath or during a nice, sensual massage. Here's an exercise to practice this.

WELCOME TO YOUR BODY

In this exercise, you will practice physically meeting and appreciating your body.

Start by rubbing your arms. Feel gratitude for their working condition.

Next, feel your breasts. Feel gratitude for the life-giving beauty of your breasts, no matter what size they are.

Rub your hands over your womb space and feel the magic of knowing that life could be created here.

Rub them over your yoni, which is your center of creativity and pleasure. Acknowledge when your cycle comes (whether you know the exact date or not) and consider that your period is a beautiful act of your body, one of many miraculous signs that you are alive.

Rub your hands down and up your legs and experience how grateful you are that your legs move you.

Finally, spend some time — as long as you like — just

breathing in your body and reveling in your intimate and sensual beauty.

Having Firm Boundaries

The sexually free woman has determined for herself when it is acceptable to have sex and when it isn't. No one else sets these boundaries for her. After my years of drunken sex ended, I settled on two major boundaries for myself:

- I have to be sober — not under the influence of any drugs or alcohol — because those substances distort my perception and impair my decision-making abilities.
- I sleep only with people with whom I have an emotional and spiritual connection. Sex is the ultimate act of receiving, and I'm receiving all my partner's energy and being during sex, so why would I want someone in my body with whom I don't feel an emotional and spiritual connection?

If one or neither of those conditions is in place, then it's not a sex match for me. Mainly, the sex is just way better and I love myself more when I am conscious, present, and aware. Disconnected sex is not goddess sex. Not bad or wrong, mind you, but not goddess sex. Goddess sex is sacred, elevated, and spiritual.

You may have similar boundaries to mine or completely different ones. If you haven't defined them in your mind, it's time to create your own boundaries, ones that feel good and true to you. Do you not want to have sex under the influence of anything? Does it feel good to commit to not sleeping with anyone on the first date? Do you want to decide not to have sex until you're in a relationship or until you're married? Whatever your boundaries are, make sure they're created *by you*, never by anyone else (not even me), and that they feel absolutely right to you.

Honoring Your "No"

Sister, you do not need to justify why you don't want to go on a date with him. You do not need to justify why you don't want to sleep with him. The answer is no, period. Stand firm in your no and don't feel like you need to come up with any excuses or reasons. Your no is your reason.

I've exercised this muscle of saying no. It happened just the other day, when a guy reached out and asked me repeatedly and persistently if he could take me out on a date. What I texted back was: "No." No reason and no, I do not need to explain myself. I had been polite several times, but still he pursued, and I wanted to be ultra clear. Believe me, guys will respect you for this, and the ones who don't respect you for it are *not* men you want in your life. How a man reacts to no can be very telling about who he truly is. When you say no for yourself, you will have so much more respect for yourself, too.

Facing and Healing Your Past

As we've seen in this chapter, it can be really difficult to recollect trauma from the past, but to be willing to go there, to shine the light on your shame and seek your own healing, makes you a woman of strength. It will help you to see and understand that you are not defined by your past.

For so long, I felt disgusting. I called myself a slut, I called myself a whore. When I started dating my first serious boy-friend at twenty-one and he requested that I be monogamous, I thought, "How am I going to do that?" It actually didn't feel possible. I was on autopilot and hadn't faced any of my past issues; I felt out of control. When I finally faced my past and worked with coaches and energy healers to bring this stuff to light, I made progress.

I encourage you to find a coach, find a therapist, or find an energy healer whom you're willing to dig deep with into whatever you need to heal from the past. It will help you so, so much.

Embodying Your Unique Expression of Sexy

This is in the title of this book: to be empowered, sexy, and free! But there is no right or wrong way to be sexy. You can do it in many ways. For me:

- I feel sexy when I go to Pilates classes and really get into my body and feel my strength.
- I feel sexy when I nourish myself with intentional food and make the effort for cooking and preparation.
- I feel sexy when I adorn myself and choose clothes that align with my self-expression and joy.

What makes you feel sexy? It's good to unleash it! Be fully in your body. Take a dance class (I love salsa dancing), or swim in a lake, or wander through a garden, or stand out in the wind in a frilly dress with a long skirt, or put on your most body-con outfit and gaze lovingly at yourself in the mirror — do whatever it takes to feel like the sexiest version of you. Face the mirror, look yourself in the eyes, and tell yourself that you love you. I know this sounds cheesy, but it is a powerful act. If you embrace your own beauty and your own body, you will be the truly empowered, sexy, and free woman that you want to be.

Whatever makes you feel sexiest, do that thing every day.

My story of my sexual past has always been the hardest to share, but it has also brought me the most freedom to claim. As my story has brought me to the present moment, I've really come into my own, feeling safe to be a woman.

Practice embodying the five traits of the sexy woman. Get help and support when you need it. The dark places are there so that you can learn to shine light on them. Remember, you were born to be a sexual being. Your desires, kinks, sexual fantasies, and sexual preferences are all a spiritual part of you; accept them fully, even if the people you love cannot. Give yourself permission to enjoy your body like you never have before. Divine, radiant woman, you are the most beautiful part of human creation. Own that.

CHAPTER EIGHT

I Embrace My

Soul Contracts

*I*magine this: One day you wake up and you find yourself on a deserted island. No people around, just you and nature. At first, you may find this fun, freeing, and relaxing, but after a while you get bored and lonely, right?

Now imagine being alone on the island for a year. A full year with no human contact, no conversation, no interaction. By the end of that year, you would start to forget who you are.

Think about that for a second. If you were on a deserted island with nobody around, you would have a very limited view of who you are, and the longer you were there, the less of yourself you'd be truly aware of.

Why? Because we are created in our relationships with the other people in our lives. The Nguni Bantu language of Southern Africa calls this *ubuntu*, which loosely translates to "I am because of you" or "People are people because of other people." In other words, your relationships are the sacred arena in which you grow into your fullest Self.

In the Western world, we don't usually see it this way. We relate to relationships as things to work on. To us, they seem confusing, even chaotic or fearful. Sometimes we wish we could get out of the relationships we have. Other times we wish we had more relationships to begin with. Almost all the time, we wish ours were somehow different.

That makes sense — we are all dynamic beings with intricate, complex subconscious minds. We're all trying to figure ourselves out. It seems counterintuitive, maybe even dangerous, to look to other people to do that. After all, we didn't *choose* them to be in our lives. Why should they and not we ourselves be the ones to shape us?

But this is where we're wrong. In reality, we did choose them. Everyone who enters our lives was someone we chose to meet in this lifetime and made an agreement with to guide us to our fullest growth.

Huh?

Yes, you may be a bit confused right now. That's okay.

This is one of my favorite spiritual concepts, and when I first learned it, it definitely seemed a little out there to me. I came across it in one of my journeys with a spiritual master, and I will never forget it. Here's how I understood it.

In the spirit plane, when you were energy waiting to take human form, your soul interviewed and conversed with thousands of other souls. You found the ones that would teach you the most and help you grow most fully, and you made contracts with these souls to show up in one another's human lives and learn from one another.

These soul contracts are behind all the relationships we have — especially the most difficult ones, for in them we have the most to learn and the most space to grow.

Some of you may be saying, "There is *no way* I chose my dad, mom, or ex-boyfriend." I want to remind you that you actually did, according to this theory (which I wholeheartedly believe). On the level of your soul, you knew that this person would help you grow, so you chose them, and they also chose you. The agreement was mutual, no matter how impossible that seems when you look at a current troubled relationship.

I used to be confused when people referred to close relationships as "reflections." As I began to understand soul contracts, I suddenly got it: these most meaningful (and sometimes most painful) relationships teach us by holding up a mirror. In them, we see our areas of greatest glory — and of our greatest need for growth.

Maybe you've been in a romantic relationship and have seen a reflection of yourself that you do not like. Maybe you showed up as clingy, needy, attached, dramatic, jealous, distant, or detached. This sacred container is showing you what is left to heal. Maybe the lesson is to dive into deeper realms of self-love, so you are not looking outside of yourself to find happiness and fulfillment.

If not a romantic partnership, maybe for you it was a relationship with a coworker, a boss, a sibling, a friend, or a parent. My own number one relationship of resistance was my mom.

Mothers and Soul Contracts

You came to planet Earth to have a human experience as a spiritual being. Taking a body gave form to the infiniteness of your soul. As mentioned before, when you entered your mother's womb you essentially became her. From birth to age seven in your developmental cycle, you were merged with her nervous system, her emotions, her experience of this life. In essence, you *were* her.

A child does not know their body as separate from their mother's; they don't know their reality as separate from their mother's.

My thousands of committed hours in transformational and healing work, as well as my personal studies of humanity and culture, have taught me about the development of the human psyche. I have turned over every stone to know my own psyche and then those of my clients.

The mother-daughter dynamic is the most complex of all human relationships; therefore, it gives us enormous data about ourselves.

In my spiritual path, I've come to be certain that nothing in this human experience is an accident or a fluke or a mistake. I believe that we chose our parents because they were the exact people who would bring us to the lessons we came to learn in this lifetime.

The mission on planet Earth is simple: to expand your soul. For better or for worse, the mama you chose was exactly whom you needed to help you carry out your spiritual growth.

If you're anything like me, your mom was not someone you would intentionally hire as your life coach. Our relationship was troubled from the start, and as an adult, I was really challenged in how I showed up for her. With my friends, I was funny, patient, kind, loving, and sweet. With my mom I was judgmental, rude, snappy, easily embarrassed, and unkind. I would often leave her house upset and flustered, wishing that she would just be different. I felt like a fraud in my life, and the anguish of being out of alignment made the difficulty of dealing with her even worse.

Understanding my soul contract with my mom changed everything. I realized that out of the thousands, maybe millions, of souls I had interviewed to be my human mother, this was the one I had chosen. And not only that, but she had also chosen me!

I was so moved when I found this teaching. I had been in tremendous resistance to my mom, questioning why she was the way that she was, wishing it were different — until I realized that she was exactly the woman I needed as my mother for my soul's highest growth in this lifetime. All the others had said no (or weren't the right ones for me to ask), but she'd said yes. Talk about a whole new level of gratitude!

Now I know that my mom has been my greatest teacher. She showed me new depths of myself, reflections that no one else would have been able to. For this, and because she is the one who brought me to this planet, I deeply honor our relationship.

To help you fully understand the complexity of my (and any) mother-daughter relationship, I'll tell you about how our relationship and place in the family felt incredibly painful to me until I was able to resolve them. First, meet my mom.

My mom was a petite beauty with a California tan and long blonde hair to her waist, rocking the seventies freedom vibes. Born in 1950, she grew up as a minister's daughter, moving around her entire childhood as her father established Christian churches in different places. She was deeply committed to the morals of Christianity and to Jesus, and she grew up indoctrinated with a strong belief in a judgmental God. Yet she also had an undeniable rebellious spirit and dreamed of a bigger life. She came of age during the countercultural revolution, the Vietnam antiwar movement, and the embracing of the hippie lifestyle.

I remember her as sweetly naive, yet aware. By the time she was in her midthirties, my mom was desperate to be a mother, but her boyfriend of eight years wouldn't commit. She told me the story of her love, Kelly: she asked him to "shit or get off the pot," and he chose to get off the pot. He left her deeply heart-broken.

Meanwhile, my mom's best friend was going through an ugly divorce with a serial cheater. Her divorce attorney was a handsome, intelligent, and respectable Marine vet, rough around the edges. One day he came across a photo of my mom. They had met only in passing a few times, and then she had left California to tend to her ailing parents. He told my mom's friend to call my mom and give her this message: "Tell Lynn to move back to California, and I'll marry her."

When she got the message, my mom was both shocked and delighted. She could finally have a husband and become a mother! She said yes, having no idea what she was really signing up for.

Within three months, they were married, and she became pregnant with my older brother. I believe that my mom's desperation to have kids as they both approached forty was, in her mind, her last chance to fulfill her dream (and my father's) of having a family. But not long after, my mom discovered that my father had a serious drug addiction, acquired while he was a fighter pilot in the Vietnam War.

Three years after my brother came along, after many attempts and one miscarriage, they had me. During my mom's pregnancy, my dad was in the throes of his addiction, fueled by his war PTSD. Later in life, my mom told me stories of his paranoia. He'd rip their house apart looking for recording devices from the government. He boarded up all the windows.

One night, the neighbors called the police because he was disturbing the peace in the neighborhood. He spent many nights in various LA County jail cells, but he was always released when they found out he was a Vietnam veteran. My mother held on to hope of his healing throughout her pregnancy, even though she felt very alone and afraid of him.

My mom had me by scheduled C-section, alone at the hospital, when I was born on June 9, 1989. The nurses called my dad to pick her up. When he arrived, he was driving a race car with all the seats except the driver's torn out of the car (this makes for a lighter car while racing). My mom held her C-section wound, her brand-new baby girl, and her three-year-old baby boy as she crawled onto the tin floor of the car and braced herself for the ride home.

Some seriously traumatic things happened to my mom and the rest of my family during the first few years of my life. She disclosed even more details as I matured and could handle the truth. Some of the memories she revealed were:

- My dad driving on the wrong side of the road on the freeway in a meth-induced mania, screaming that he was going to kill the entire family
- My dad revealing to my mom that he had no money to pay for the food they'd just ordered at a café and telling her she would need to wash dishes to pay for the meal
- My dad's criminal clients paying him in stolen cars, which they left in front of the house, and the police coming to retrieve the cars
- My dad telling my mom that I was not his child and accusing her of adultery
- The bartender of a local bar calling my mom to tell

> her that my dad was drunk and her three-year-old
> son was wandering the bar alone

I know there were other things that happened that my mom never had the courage to tell me — abuse that was too painful for her to ever recount.

The grand finale came when my mom fled the house with both kids while my dad was in a state of paranoid mania. Because he believed that the house was bugged by the government, he instructed his criminal clients to completely empty our home. My mom sent friends over to retrieve her belongings, but it was too late. Her pictures, her childhood memorabilia, her books, her trunk of keepsakes, her furniture, her clothes — everything she owned was gone.

This was the final straw. My mom boarded a flight with my toddler brother and me, a baby in her arms, without a dollar to her name. She went to her dad's one-bedroom house in Michigan. At forty, she was completely shattered and terrified for her life, and had to humble herself to asking her elderly father for help.

She was granted a restraining order against my dad, and they didn't speak for many months. She felt like an absolute failure, having to disclose to her extremely conservative Christian minister father what was actually happening with her husband, a secret she had been keeping from him. She told me the stories of barely having enough money to eat and buy diapers and of having to rely on the generosity of the church to support her and her children.

When I think of what she went through, I feel a sense of grief and anguish that breaks my heart. All my mom ever wanted was a Christian family, a simple life in California, a loving place to feel safe. And she married a man who was deeply tormented from the war, unable to get a grip on his resulting drug addiction.

My mom had to return to California a few times to show up in court for custody and divorce proceedings. She saw him in the lobby of the courtroom, a shattered shell of a human wearing torn shoes and eating a PB&J sandwich from a plastic baggie, and all she wanted to do was save him and make him better. But she knew she couldn't. His addiction was far greater than both of them at the time.

During the last trip back to California to finalize the divorce, my parents' attorneys arranged a meeting so my dad could see me and my brother. They agreed to meet in public, at the *Queen Mary* in Long Beach. As the tale is told, my brother ran to my dad screaming, "Daddy!!," elated to see his beloved father again. We spent the afternoon feeding the ducks, my parents trying to make sense of what our family was.

My dad explained to my mom that he had been sober for months and had recommitted his life to Jesus. His aunt had welcomed him into her trailer home, where he had detoxed. He swore to Mom on his life that he would never touch meth again; he would show up as the father and husband she needed him to be (and he did keep his word).

My mother canceled the restraining order and the divorce, and there we were, a family of four reunited. Many people wouldn't have risked it, but my mom believed in him and his spiritual reconciliation. As older parents, they were restarting a family and marriage from ground zero, with debt, ruined credit, and just a few dollars to their names. They rented a small apartment in the suburbs of San Diego, and we restarted our lives, as a united family, the Pinkertons.

My dad no longer had a driver's license, so he rode the trolley to work in downtown San Diego, and he rebuilt his career as an attorney. I don't have many pictures of myself as a baby, since they were all destroyed in the house clearing, but I do have photographs from the apartment days as a two-year-old, all dressed up in my pink dress and frilly white tights, holding on to my brother in his button-up shirt as we headed to church on Sundays.

My mom and dad both worked to try to rebuild their finances, living one day at a time. My mom told me stories of having not a dollar to their names to buy dinner, and then magically she would get a call from a massage client and earn forty dollars that would pay for dinner that night. My dad stayed sober, and they were able to slowly get ahead financially. By the time I was two years old, my parents had saved up enough money to buy a house in a remote mountain town near San Diego, an hour inland from the coast. They chose a house far away from LA, my dad's old circle of friends, and their previous life.

It was in this house that I saw my mother's dreams crushed.

My mom adored Los Angeles. She loved the beach, and she loved the happenings of a big city. Though she was grateful for our home and our life as a family, a piece of her soul died in those traumatic meth years, and she never restored that part of herself. I truly believe that my mom's relationship with my dad was built on trauma, distrust, and pain. She said that he never apologized for what he had done and denied that most of it ever happened. He was probably protecting himself, but it caused a rift between them. In Los Angeles, my mom had had a promising career as a Christian singer. She'd had all the right connections, an agent, and one of the most angelic voices ever heard. All of this was taken from her when she lived deep in the mountains, in a town full of country farming folk whom she never quite resonated with.

My brother and I knew this fact as we were growing up: that Mom didn't want to be in this town. She told stories of the magical field of LA, but we had to be here for Dad's sake and because it was where we could afford to own our home.

When parents have trauma, children have trauma, and when a mother in particular has trauma, so does her daughter. Over the next five years, I developed a debilitating shyness and selective mutism. I was extremely fearful of other people and the world. I remember being very aware of adults when I was in preschool and wishing intensely that I could be in their world and part of their conversations; the kids my age scared me. I never slept during nap time, always hypervigilant and eavesdropping on the adult conversations. I developed a thumb-sucking habit when I saw two of my friends doing it, and this self-soothing habit followed me into adulthood.

When I was five, I started kindergarten. I distinctly remember this part of my life. The kindergarten playground was separated from the older kids' playground by a circular dome of bars. One day I held on to the bars and peered out toward the big kids' area. To the best of my ability, I calculated on my fingers how many years it would take me to become a sixth grader. I couldn't do the exact math, but I knew that it was more fingers than time I wanted to wait. I looked at the older kids, then back at the kids my age as they were gleefully playing with toys, swinging, and riding tricycles. I remember saying to myself, "I don't want to play, I don't belong here, I can't wait until I'm older," and thinking about how long I was going to have to be trapped in a child's body. It was a daunting feeling. (Today, I consider this a distinct memory of the moment I realized I had reincarnated and would have to do childhood over again.)

Thirty minutes from our house there was a casino on a Native reservation, and my dad introduced my mom to the pastime of gambling. They dabbled in drinking and gambling and were frequent travelers to Las Vegas. I remember lots of fighting in the home; many times I was embarrassed that my friends witnessed the ferocious fights.

As I grew older, I suffered from extreme anxiety, self-doubt, and severe inhibition, and I learned to hide my pain and my true self. I also realized I could use my logic to outsmart authority and that if I stayed hyperaware, I would be safer. I was in a mad race to reach maturity so I could feel safe in the world, and I developed a huge unconscious pressure to grow up quickly and succeed. I learned to hide the secrets about my family and put on a happy face, pretending that everything was normal and okay.

I was highly sensitive, and I remember a few times having to be picked up from school because I was hyperventilating from crying after my teacher lightly disciplined me. I was wounded and traumatized. And deep inside, part of me held my mother responsible.

But what if she and I had made a soul contract? With all she suffered and all I suffered, this changes everything about who was responsible and why it all happened. I think about this a lot; recognizing this was part of the reason why I initiated the medicine journey experience I told you about in chapter 4.

Your Soul Contracts

Chances are, dear one, that you had some level of a harsh entrance into this world. You more than likely came into a family that didn't fully recognize your sensitivities and light, didn't fully provide you the safety and security you needed to develop healthy self-esteem. It's not that they were a bad family. It's just that people see the world through their own lenses, which often don't reflect anyone else's truth. We are all wounded in some way, and to become whole, we need to see it and acknowledge it and integrate it into our consciousness.

I wish none of us had to go back and experience the pain we felt in early childhood. I wish I could tell you that there is another way through, but that's not how the laws of physics work. Physics tells us that energy is never created nor destroyed, only transmuted. We cannot destroy the pain that happened to you as a child, but we can transmute it into usable energy. And believe me, it is most definitely what has built your character and made you the strong, compassionate woman you are today. After all, if these lessons were part of your soul contract, then they all happened for a reason.

ASK YOURSELF

How does it feel to consider that *you* are the ultimate creator of your experience and that everyone in your life is there because you chose them to be? Does this ignite any feelings for you? Do you feel empowered? Or triggered? (Maybe a little of both?)

If you're feeling triggered or confused, ask yourself:

- What am I not wanting to see?
- Is it scary to think that I am the creator of my life the way it is right now?
- What would that mean about how powerful I actually am?
- What would it mean about the choices and soul contracts that I've made?
- Who are my most important relationships with?
- What have I learned from them?
- What relationships do I have in which I don't like how I show up?
- How can I be more intentional, more grateful, more truly myself with them? Consider who I am because of these people and who they might be because of me.

Be with this trigger. Honor it. It's there to help you grow. Just as I mentioned earlier — your triggers are your signals for freedom — your relationships are, too.

Relationships are a sacred container for you to enter in order to gain deeper insight into who you really are. I invite you to take a look at all the relationships in your life. Send every single person a burst of love in this moment. Bust out your journal and write the important ones down. Allow this concept to give you a whole new appreciation for your fellow humans on the planet. See everybody in your life as offering a sacred learning experience. From the woman in line at the bank to your closest family member, they are all playing a role *for you*.

The Shadow Side

One thing that I want you to be clear about is that knowing people are in your life to help you grow doesn't mean that you are "nice" to everyone and play the little fairy goddess role to people whom you know may hurt you or diminish you. I used to do this. I would say, "Ah, I love people, we are all one, no one will ever harm me." I cut off my awareness and chose not to see the shadow side of people — and got burned. Everyone has a shadow side to varying degrees, make no mistake.

Think of scorpions, for example. They're perfectly wonderful creatures, essential to the ecosystem, but it is in their nature to sting. You can admire them and be around them, but it is best not to get too close.

If you think about it, you'll know who the scorpions are in your life. Maybe they have agreed to play this role with you so that you can learn to set your boundaries and honor your no. This may be a difficult friend who keeps betraying your trust. You can still love her as a human being, but you may not want her to be a close person in your life.

This Sanskrit fable, which is viral online, describes the scorpion nature of some people:

> A scorpion, being a very poor swimmer, asked a turtle to carry him on his back across a river.
>
> "Are you mad?" exclaimed the turtle. "You'll sting me while I'm swimming, and I'll drown."
>
> "My dear turtle," laughed the scorpion, "if I were to sting you, you would drown, and I would go down with you. Now where is the logic in that?"
>
> "You're right!" cried the turtle. "Hop on!" The scorpion climbed aboard...and halfway across the river gave the turtle a mighty sting.

As they both sank to the bottom, the turtle resignedly said: "Do you mind if I ask you something? You said there'd be no logic in your stinging me. Why did you do it?"

"It has nothing to do with logic," the drowning scorpion sadly replied. "It's just my character."

We have all had experiences with people who have bitten or stung us. You can still love that person and be incredibly grateful for them while also creating healthy boundaries. For instance, if your dad is an alcoholic and continually betrays your trust, maybe you need to not invite him to occasions where there will be alcohol, creating a boundary for yourself to keep a loving distance. Or if you have a girlfriend who continually tries to criticize you and diminish your light so she can feel better about her own insecurities, maybe your boundary looks like being explicit with her about the positive and supportive space that you would like to create with her, or maybe you choose to not make plans with her. *You* are the designer of your life; *you* are truly the ultimate creator, and you can always tap into your intuition to feel into what is best for you. Even if your soul chose to learn something from someone, you can always draw a boundary when enough is enough. Remember that soul contracts sometimes need to be updated!

As you settle into this mindset shift of relating to everyone as being partners in soul contracts you created together, be aware of what lessons certain people bring you. Honor these reflections. Treat every human like the true infinite being of light that they truly are, even if they lead with their shadow side. Be mindful of the scorpions and use your best judgment for setting your boundaries.

Remember, love, this life was set up for you, not against

you, even when it's been painful. Every single person in your life is playing the role that you assigned to them. Rise above the drama of the play to see the lesson happening behind the scenes. This is where you take all your power back. This is where you own your sexy. This is where you reclaim your freedom.

Coming up next, I am going to share with you the number one reason that our energy leaks out and diminishes our power without us realizing it. Hint: energetic leakage is all created in our relationships with others. The tool you are about to receive will forever change the way you relate and connect to other people — if you are brave enough to implement it in your life. May I take you there?

CHAPTER NINE

I Rise to Harmonious Relationships

We live in a culture of attachment. This is especially true with relationships. We tend to hold on to relationships. We stay so attached to people — we are "best friends for life" and we vow to be together "until death do us part." We're taught to stay attached at all costs, especially in romantic relationships, because this other person is what makes our lives complete.

Think about common phrases like "BFFs — best friends forever," movie quotes like "You complete me," and song lyrics like "My life would suck without you." When someone is part of our life, whether friend or partner or family member, our culture and society tell us to hold on to them no matter what!

What happens when that fails?

A longtime partner dumps you. A close friend decides they don't want to be friends anymore. A supervisor you respect fires you. A sibling sides against you in a family disagreement. Suddenly the person you were holding on to is gone, for the moment or forever. How do you handle it? You may feel heart-break, an identity crisis, or even a total meltdown.

I had an imprinting experience in my first job, when I was sixteen. I was the top in sales for a tanning salon chain in San Diego. I loved this job! I couldn't wait to go there every day, and I put so much hard work into it. I was writing the schedule by the time I was seventeen, and I made manager by eighteen. The owner and I had a really tight relationship. I saw us as having a deep connection and being friends for life. I valued everything she taught me and appreciated all the responsibilities she let me take on. I loved how much she trusted me.

Fast-forward to when I was nineteen and went to college, which was also when I got heavily into Adderall and a lot of drinking, and I developed an eating disorder because I didn't eat when I was taking amphetamines. I became a really distracted and unpredictable employee, with questionable integrity. I made it look like I was there when I wasn't. I delegated all my managerial duties to the assistant manager. Eventually I started just not showing up at all (though I always acted like I had been there). I was still close with the owner at this point, but I didn't tell her about any of my issues.

The owner eventually found out what I was doing and fired me. I was devastated, and a piece of my identity was lost that day. I remember driving away upset and crying because I had broken her trust and ruined our friendship. I felt like I had completely sabotaged our connection and she'd never let me into her life again. We didn't talk for another couple of years.

The pain and loss of that moment stayed with me for a long time. I was afraid to get another job, because what if the same thing happened again and I lost another important person I looked up to? What if I fucked things up again? Ugh, if only I hadn't been such an idiot, a druggie, an irresponsible worker, this might not have happened.

Does this thought pattern sound familiar?

It's where our heads go when the attachments that we hold closely are left incomplete — when there's more we wish we could have said or done before the relationship ended. It's the ex-boyfriend you can't stop thinking about, playing "What if…" over and over in your head. It's the argument you had with your girlfriend and the trigger you feel every time you see her picture on Facebook, especially if she looks like she's having fun without you. It's the tension you feel when you haven't talked to your mom in more than a month and the last thing she said to you has been pissing you off.

This is what I call energetic leakage, when your power and energy are leaking from you without you consciously realizing it.

The energy you want to use to move forward in your life is leaking out through the cracks of these broken, incomplete relationships that you are unable to let go of. Just as you can't hold water in a cracked bowl, you can't hold energy in a cracked spirit.

Places in your life where you are incomplete with people and hold heavy emotions about past experiences will always be a big drain on your energy. If you have someone in your past whom you left off with an argument, you left off with things unsaid, you left off with hurt and pain, you left off by saying things you regret — if there's someone with whom you wish it had ended differently — you will unconsciously focus more on the incompleteness than on moving forward with your life. You'd better believe that every time I thought about the tanning salon, emotional incompleteness hit me hard.

It feels even worse when you think the other person

wronged you and broke the relationship. Resentment and bitter indignation at having been treated unfairly are two of the greatest silent killers in our culture. You replay that scenario in your head, holding on to regret or righteous anger, wishing it had been different, planning defenses to make sure it never happens again. Your hate paralyzes you. You couldn't move forward if you wanted to.

Why can't we let go of these incomplete attachments? On some level, we know they're hurting us. Why can't we just drop them?

It's absolutely heartbreaking to me how common it is to hear, "I haven't spoken to my sister in five years" or "I haven't called my dad since we argued six months ago." I have no doubt that you have very valid reasons to feel hurt and keep a safe distance, but is angry silence ultimately what you really want out of these relationships? You may wonder why the incompleteness is itself so hard to let go of.

Often, it's because *you're holding on to some past view of yourself.* You may not like who you were in that relationship, and you are terrified to own up to it. You could be dragging who you were in your last romantic relationship with you into your new relationship. You could be lugging who you were in the past with your parents into the present. I was terrified to start a new job after I was fired because I was hauling the version of who I'd been in the salon job along with me.

Facing our past selves can feel really, really tough. But it's the only way to let go of the incomplete relationships that drag us down and sap our energy.

I had created a story in my mind that I would always have to hide what had happened at the salon and that the owner would never forgive me. I hated this past view of myself and tried to hide it, but hate and shame only locked it more firmly into place inside my energetic body. I knew I couldn't live with the energy leak forever. I had an awareness that I needed to revisit the relationship and complete it from an empowered place.

After more than two years of silence, I finally worked up my courage and called the salon owner. I explained what had been going on in my life and took responsibility for what a crappy employee I had been. She responded with loving compassion, and in just one moment, I was free from something that had been eating away at me for years. I can't tell you how much release I experienced in that moment. We even met for lunch and had a beautiful time getting caught up. I had been head tripping over conclusions I'd made up that weren't even real. And we now have a loving relationship — the kind I always wanted.

So now I want to ask you: Are there any relationships in your life right now that you're feeling incomplete with? I'm guessing there might be a few. (I once worked with a client who made a list of more than eighty!)

Maybe there's a relationship in your life that you're ready to let go of. Maybe it's a romantic relationship or your best friend who is holding you back. Maybe it's a relationship with a coworker or your job. How can you let go of the incompleteness with integrity and with ease?

First, know that no other person has the power to complete you. You are the only one who can make yourself feel complete. You are the only one who can make yourself happy. If you're relying on someone else to come do that for you, you're going to have a very rude awakening, because you'll always be in a position of waiting and feeling empty. You especially won't find it in a dysfunctional relationship from the past. Shift your focus to finding happiness in and with yourself.

Next, ask yourself: Where do you need to own up to something from the past? Where are you still playing the victim, and where can you take your power back? You say you want to be empowered. This starts in your relationships. You have to be willing to act out of integrity. Are you willing to take full ownership and responsibility? Access the purest place of your heart, cultivate forgiveness, and feel into what you really want to express.

So what do you need to clean up, sister? What have you not been willing to look at in past relationships? If there's something that's eating away at you, bugging you, continually popping up in your thoughts, then this is a red flag for you to take back your power and clean up the things that you need to clean up. (Though maybe it wouldn't be in your best interest to go digging up something with an ex whom you have a restraining order on. Be smart and be safe. Use your awareness.)

Then, reach out to the people you feel incomplete with. Talk with them about how you would like to own up to being out of integrity, how you felt during the times of conflict, what you were dealing with at the time. Offer them an apology if you feel led to.

Note: what you don't want to do when you're reaching out to somebody is to bring up the past incidents and make the other person wrong. I didn't reach out to my boss and say, "Because you weren't there all the time, I did this." It wasn't about making anybody else wrong; it was about owning up to what I had done that was out of integrity.

Finally, no matter what happens in the conversation you have with them, resolve to remember them with forgiveness.

Forgiveness will set you free. It does not mean that you condone what someone has done in the past. It simply means that you let go of the desire to make them wrong. Invoke your divine compassion. See that everyone is truly doing the best they can with the tools that they've got. If they want to reconnect with you, welcome them. If not, let them transition gracefully out of your life — without taking any more of your energy with them.

Repeat these steps with everyone whom you feel incomplete with and can safely reach out to. You'll be amazed at the peace waiting for you when you do.

To help you deepen your understanding of how this works, here are some sample conversations of completion conversations I have had in the past.

SCENARIO: My college roommate moved out abruptly after I discovered that she had been secretly sleeping with the guy I was dating. We were best friends, had *so* much fun together, and she'd introduced me to all my college friends. Instead of facing what she had done, she moved out and went back to San Francisco, completely leaving her college experience behind. Every time I thought of her, I had a terrible feeling in my stomach. Three years after she moved out, I reached out with this text:

> Hi, it's Jolie. I just have to say, I miss our connection so deeply. Every time I see an old pic of us I get so sad that you left college and we ended our friendship over a boy. I want to take responsibility for being the type of person who it was so difficult to come to and tell me. I hope that you're doing well in SF, and I would love to reconnect if you're ever in San Diego.

OUTCOME: She texted back with so much joy that I had reached out. She said, "I cannot let you take responsibility; I am so sorry for what happened." This finally completed the energetic loop that had been open for three years. I felt peace around our relationship. Notice that I did not bring up the past and make her wrong. I did not request an apology. I tapped into my deepest truth and said what my heart really wanted to say, which was that I missed her and I didn't give a shit about the boy. Now, when I see her on Facebook, I have a restored love and friendship. Success!

SCENARIO: During the end of my last relationship, my partner and I both felt dishonored in many ways. I needed some space to heal. Because my partner was female, I had brought her intimately into my sister circles of friends, and the lines were blurred. Many of my oldest friends became close to my former partner after our relationship ended.

One of my best friends of more than a decade invited my former partner to a party just weeks after we'd ended our relationship. I was planning on going to this party but didn't attend when two of my friends texted me that she was there. It hurt me tremendously, because many of my friends were at this party and I felt like I didn't have a safe space to heal. This is not typically the way I like to do relationship transitions, but I really needed space for this one.

I requested a phone call with my friend who'd invited her and said this during our conversation:

> I know you didn't mean to hurt me by inviting her to the party, but it ended up really hurting me — can I share why? I'm in a very tender place right now with

this breakup, and I need to know that my friends are here and have my back. My life had gotten very enmeshed and codependent, and I need to work on rebuilding my identity and having places to connect with my friends without the trigger of my former partner around.

OUTCOME: My friend and I had a challenging yet beautiful conversation. She understood my pain, and we were able to move on instead of harboring resentment. One thing to note here is that I said in the beginning of the conversation, "I know you didn't mean to hurt me." Oftentimes, people are going to assume that they are in trouble and listen to you from a defensive place, especially if they think they did something wrong. Try saying something at the beginning of the conversation to let them know that this is not a fight, a confrontation, or a sticky conversation. You can start with a compliment, an acknowledgment of their innocent intentions, and an insight as to why you are reaching out.

Imagine how much ease and grace you will have in your life when you have completed all your past relationships and attachments. You will not be scared to run into a certain person randomly, nor have anxiety around seeing each other at a mutual friend's party, nor have to avoid anyone. Tap into your purest heart space and express what is truly there for you. You will be surprised how expanded and peaceful you will feel after you have these completion conversations. You will restore your energy and return to your natural inner brilliance.

I invite you to put these tools into action and start implementing what you're learning in this book, if you haven't already. Begin by making your list of people and bravely initiate your completion conversations. Remember, everything you want for yourself is on the other side of fear. All the sexiness, power, and freedom you could ever imagine are waiting for you when you're willing to step outside of your comfort zone. I'm proud of you! You can do this!

The next chapter is essential to our healing process together and was by far the most challenging chapter for me to write: it is about healing your relationship with God. You can repair energy leakages by releasing attachment, but to really seal them off may take some divine intervention. I will share with you my journey into discovering who God really is for me and my story of embracing a spiritual path. This is the core of our process together. An intimate relationship with the divine is the sexiest relationship you will ever have in this lifetime.

CHAPTER TEN

I Am at One with God

I spent so many years completely shut down spiritually that even now I don't always feel worthy or ready to write about my connection with the divine. I do know that healing my relationship with God allowed me to reach the most blissful experiences of my life and totally access my unique brilliance and purpose. But talking about it is still really tough. It brings up mental questions like: "Who the heck am I to write about this?" "Who will listen to someone with my past talking about God?" "*God* is such a trigger word anyway — will people even want to read this chapter?" and "People have been asking, 'What is God?' and 'Why are we here?' for centuries. Why would I have any answers?"

Writing about God is incredibly complex, so let me just start with what is real for me: my own experience.

As I mentioned earlier, I grew up in a very strict Christian household. Yes, I know — people grow up in those households all the time and have happy, empowered lives in which they can connect easily with God and spirituality. Maybe you're one of those people. If so, you are blessed, and I celebrate you. But this wasn't the case for me.

In my understanding of the world through religion, everything was right or wrong, black or white, heaven or hell. There wasn't any space in my family to really explore spirituality on my own or find my own expression of it. Sunday school taught me that I was wrong for questioning God, and that's just the way things were. When I was confused and sometimes scared by my own religion, I felt even more wrong for feeling those things.

It was disempowering, to say the least. I was in a select group that was going to heaven when everyone else was going to hell, and my job was to convince others to believe what I believed. It was so much work, I felt like I was pushing a huge boulder uphill trying to convince people that life was a certain way. And I couldn't even really convince myself. My agnostic friends were going to hell, my Mormon friends were doing it wrong, the Catholics were strange for honoring Mary...I couldn't believe that was the way things really worked, that I was in a chosen club of sorts and others weren't. But I also felt wrong for wanting to challenge that belief system or just trying to figure out another way that worked for me.

I've come a long way since then and made peace with my relationship with God as I grappled with my sexuality and my spirituality, as I explained before. Now I want to ask you: Are you wondering how you can find and heal your own connection with God? You may be curious to redefine what you think of as God. Maybe you don't know where to start. Maybe you've still got some triggers or blocks around God or church or spirituality or even some of the things I've said here, in these pages.

That's all right.

The first step is to work through this topic and explore it on your own terms. This is your life, your being, not anyone else's, so you get to decide how you do it.

Here's my favorite example of that. One major issue for me was that, as I started healing my relationship with God, I had so many triggering thoughts around the word *God*. I pictured this man with gray hair, wearing a robe and sitting up in heaven, and I pictured him mad at me. I pictured him upset, telling me everything that I had done wrong, dousing me with shame and judgment.

What really helped me at first was that for a long time, whenever I talked or thought about anything spiritual, *I didn't use the word* God. It had so much added meaning to it, I just wasn't comfortable using it right away. This is a common trigger for people in our situation — you might hear people use terms like "source energy" or "the universe" or just "infinite love." Whatever vocabulary speaks to you, use it.

You can do the same with any other religious words that trigger you: *prayer, spirit, church, Father, Jesus, communion, sin, salvation, gratitude,* and so on. Find the language that works for you.

I also eventually stopped thinking of God as a person at all. For us to think that God is a man and try to humanize him with human judgments and concerns is limiting. I believe that God is much greater than this. All we have to do is look at nature to see God everywhere in this human experience. Just look down at your body right now and understand the trillions of cells working together in harmony to make you a human being. Look at a pregnant woman and just consider the concept of giving birth to life! *That* is God. That is the magnificent creator! The hand that wrote you is the hand that writes it all.

The other important step is to get the support you need from the people you want it from. Maybe these are members of your church. Maybe they're members of a completely different church. Maybe they are your family or close friends or counselors or therapists. Maybe they're priests or pastors or yogis or enlightened masters.

Taking the first steps was scary for me. I was bumping into many fears because I was going up against everything my family had taught me for my whole childhood. But I had support from people who had the kind of spiritual life I wanted — they were living free of toxic shame, empowered, creating what looked like miracles every day, in touch with being inseparable from God. And with their help, I started my own spiritual path, and it's been worth every step.

So that's the beginning of the how. But what about the why? Why would you even want to do this? Why did I want to come back, after running away from it for so long?

Healing your connection with God, finding the kingdom of heaven within you, is the key to both your personal peace and the world's.

We as a human species have been trying to answer questions like "Why are we here?," "What is the meaning of life?," and "What does this all mean?" since the beginning of time. I believe the answers to those questions lie in finding and healing our spiritual connections. The greatest thinkers talk about doing this through a spiritual awakening, which is truly realizing that you are a spirit in a human body having a human experience because there is something here for you to learn. Before this awakening, it's easy to believe we are limited by our humanity, to feel trapped by it. We forget that while we came here to have a human experience, that experience does not define us. (This is why going out in nature and expanding your mind can be such a pure and powerful way to access God — it reminds us of the great creative power and presence from which we came and to which we'll someday return.)

This is the most crucial point I want to make in the entire book: If you desire to find your unique brilliance, you don't have to try nearly as hard to find it when you're connected to your spiritual source. It just IS you.

If you're willing to realize that there's something so much greater here — that there is a design, a script that has been magnificently crafted just for you, in your own uniqueness and in your own divine purpose — you will understand there is nobody like you on the entire planet. Your purpose is to be that person that is you, and healing your connection to God will dramatically ease this process.

Now I think that I have some grasp of what God is. To me, it is the glue that holds this entire creation together, the intelligence that causes everything to come together with divine perfection. God is the magic that makes a fetus become a real human. God is the magic that keeps the ocean unified in perfect balance. God is gravity, God is an orgasm, God is love. And you are this magic. You are inseparable from the magical brilliance of God.

Here is something I wrote in my journal:

I'm not really sure how or why this universe works. I don't know what infinity means, and I cannot wrap my head around how a heart beats. All I know is that I feel connected to something far greater than this planet and our solar system. I do not think God is meant to be put into language. I think it is an energy that can only be felt and experienced. I know it is not an acci-dent that I am alive right now, at this time in history, in this body, with these soul contracts. I am here to do something great. I am here to leave a legacy. Univer-sal source energy, God, all creation — use me. I am ready to fully embrace all the gifts you have given me. Show me how my fellow humans need me, and I will serve. I surrender to this magical place. I will follow.

Ever since I wrote this, pure magic has been coming to me. The people who have supported me in advancing my journey are magnetized to me. I don't have to go out searching. I've found a deep clarity and sense of direction. And, most impor-tantly, I'm having more fun.

It's Time to Go Deeper

So how can you get started on a spiritual path or deepen your current practice? If you want to connect to your spirituality, your intuition, and your divine potential and you're ready to release control and allow yourself to be guided, let's get you started. Maybe you've tried to take up a spiritual practice be-fore — meditation, yoga, reading all the books — and whatever you've tried hasn't worked. Maybe you've gotten dissatisfied with the whole thing and come to me (or someone like me) to help you find the right way to do it.

Sister, I've got some bad news for you.

There is no "right" way to connect to the divine. There is no one way that is better than any other. It is solely based on *you* and how *you* feel. If what you did before didn't work, then it wasn't the right thing for you, or else you weren't looking at it the right way, as something you chose rather than something someone was supposed to do for you. Beautiful soul, no master, book, or workshop will ever be able to do it for you. You must make the choice to become at one with God for yourself — no one else can do that for you.

Why? Because the relationship you seek with the divine is actually the relationship you seek with yourself.

Whatever you perceive as the divine — God, another deity, spirit, the universe, the earth, anything else — created you. You are a part of the creator, and the creator is a part of you, just as a mother is part of her children and a child is part of their mother. To love the divine is to love yourself, and to love yourself is to love the divine.

Maybe you're thinking that spirituality means being a hippie and burning incense and never showering and talking in big words that no one understands. Um...maybe? If that's your thing? But if it's not, then no.

I remember attending a sound healing event once and looking around at everyone, thinking they had completely lost their minds. I was so uncomfortable. Everyone was all airy-fairy and overly scented with essential oil. I couldn't focus on what I was there to learn. Everyone was having a powerful experience, and I just wanted out.

Have you ever felt that uncomfortable around other people's spirituality?

I had to ask myself: Why was I so triggered? It took me a while to understand what was going on, but eventually I realized I was being shown that I was not comfortable in *my own* expression of spirituality. To me, spirituality was right only if

it was done in secrecy. Maybe I wasn't totally into sound healing, or maybe I was, but what was really bothering me was the
openness of it all. Such an open expression of spirituality made
me really uncomfortable, even though I'd chosen to be there in
the first place.

But the more I thought about it, the more I understood
that spirituality is a unique expression for each of us. However
you like to connect to something that's greater than you, to divinity in whatever form you envision, is perfect.

For me this means that I don't have to dress a certain way,
talk a certain way, or pray a certain way to be "spiritual." I still
love my sexy little black dress collection; I *love* adorning myself
with makeup and jewelry. The difference now is that when I
adorn myself, I do it from the knowledge that I'm already perfect, beautiful, and complete. I do not use something outside of
myself to feel beautiful, any more than I use something outside
of myself to feel spiritual. I love connecting to source; it makes
me feel a profound sense of belonging and connectedness in
this world. I remember that loving divinity means loving myself, and vice versa.

It's not always easy, for me or for any of us. Somewhere
along the way, we forgot that we chose the bodies we're in because they were and are exactly what we need to carry out our
divine mission. We judge the crap out of our bodies, starve
ourselves, compare ourselves, and constantly wish we were different. And then we try to love ourselves at the same time! Not
a very comfortable space to be in.

How do you stay out of that space? By practicing awareness
and choice. By being conscious that you are doing something
and choosing something different.

Remember the chapters on triggers (chapter 3) and ego
(chapter 4)? We talked about being aware of our thoughts and

feelings as they show up and identifying them as functions of our minds rather than reflections of our selves. We also talked about consciously choosing to experience joy over sadness, relaxation over tension, and so forth. These same practices will help you see and love your own divinity and spirituality, even when you don't feel like you can or want to. (Feel free to refer back to those two chapters if you need to!)

Here are some other practices that can help as well:

- DEVELOP A CONSISTENT PRACTICE. Whatever you commit to, whether it be meditation, journaling, chanting, praying, singing, yoga, or gardening, do it consistently. Do it with joy. Allow yourself to find the pleasure of the practice. They say it takes twenty-one days to form a new habit, so give yourself those three weeks. If one practice doesn't work for you, try another. Remember, there's no wrong way to get spiritual.

- LOOK INTO THE EYES OF YOUR FELLOW HUMANS. Really. It's called eye gazing, and I love it. I was so freaked out by this practice initially. It can be a bit uncomfortable at first to see and be seen so vulnerably. But let me tell you, when you are able to quiet your mind and then gaze into another human's eyes, you will find a spiritual beauty that can move you to tears. The eyes are the gateway to the soul. Allow yourself to experience the resonance, the wonderment, the curiosity of what those eyes have seen. There is always so much more than what you see on the surface. (Note: this is best done either with a close friend or in an eye-gazing event, at least at first.)

- **STAY IN GRATITUDE.** Being grateful expands your vibration, makes your energy field lighter, and allows you to attract what you desire with ease. It lets the universe know that you're happy to be here. It reminds *you* that you're happy to be here.

- **LIVE BEYOND THIS PHYSICAL DIMENSION.** When I first worked with an energy healer, it completely shook up my reality. She could see things that I couldn't: my energetic body, my aura, my chakra system. You don't have to be able to see these things to know that they are there. Live beyond the confines of this reality, whatever that means for you. Speak to your angels, request support from your guides, honor the mystery beyond what meets the eye.

- **BE AWARE OF YOUR VIBRATION.** A mind filled with doubt, worry, regret, resentment, jealousy, or anger will affect your vibration. We all know the Negative Nancy — when she enters the room, we feel a shift. We can all feel the tightening. Be responsible for your vibration. Cultivate a mind filled with peace, love, possibility, light, and joy! You will be the light in the room that magnetically attracts others.

- **LOVE YOURSELF WITH ALL YOU'VE GOT.** How much love do you have for yourself? Are you willing to fall into a deep romance with yourself? I challenge you to look in the mirror, look into your own eyes, just as you are and as you're not, and say, "I love you" ten times every day. This will completely alter your vibration. In this practice, you are honoring yourself as divinity, as the light itself. See beauty and perfection in your own eyes. See the infinite, divine being that you truly are.

The most important thing to remember is that you truly are the creator of your life experience. Do not let your mind go on autopilot, especially if you're about to enter a situation you know may be triggering. Activate your awareness and choice. Allow yourself to cultivate and nurture a deep relationship with the divine. When you do, you will feel bliss like you've never felt before. Homecoming, contentment, ease, pleasure, and release — all these wonderful things and more are waiting for you.

You are a spiritual being having a human experience, not the other way around. The only thing that is real in this human experience is love. Are you creating love for yourself and your life? Are you allowing the divine spirit of love to fill you and fuel you? What would it take for you to feel deserving of the abundance of love waiting for you? It's yours to claim. In love, you are free.

CHAPTER ELEVEN

I Am

Presence

Our current cultural system is set up so there is always somewhere to go and something to accomplish before we can be truly happy and enjoy life.

Kindergarten leads to first grade. Grade school leads to high school. High school leads to college leads to graduate school leads to a job. Job leads to promotion leads to seniority leads to retirement. Dating leads to engagement leads to marriage leads to kids leads to grandkids. You may skip some of these steps, but *there is always a next step.*

Wherever we are, our focus is on getting to the *next* thing. Once we get there, happiness awaits...or so we are told. I get this all the time when I walk into Nordstrom — it's a gigantic display of all the amazing things I don't have yet! As soon as I can save up enough to get that purse, I'll be happy, right?

You know where I'm going with this, don't you? You've felt it yourself — the moment when you get to that next place or you buy that next thing and you realize you aren't any happier than you were before you got it. Maybe you're feeling that way right now.

Or maybe you're feeling that where you are is so hard, so tiring, to intolerable, that *any* next thing has got to be better. Sister, I'm with you. For me that time came right after college, when I watched dream jobs fall into all my friends' laps while I received rejection letter after rejection letter.

It's great to have desires. It's great to have goals. It's great to know where you want to go. But your true fulfillment and joy don't come from those things. And the more I dwelled on the things I didn't have, the places I hadn't gotten to yet, the farther from those things I felt.

The truth is, we can never really escape ourselves. Wherever you go, there you'll be. You can travel, you can get a new job, you can switch towns, you can get a new house or car or boyfriend, but if you're not settled and present within yourself, you'll never be able to escape needing the next thing.

To truly find your brilliance, to truly be empowered and free, you must shift your focus from the future to the present. Instead of dwelling on what you don't have, be willing to cultivate a sense of arrival into the now, a feeling of pure excitement and gratitude for what *is*. This is the art of arrival.

To me, *arrival* is a synonym for *presence*. You're not stuck somewhere in the past, nor are you rushing ahead to get to something in the future. You are here, now. Your arrival in this moment acknowledges that you are exactly where you need to be and what you have is enough. Knowing this, you are able to look around and experience the wonderment and the magic of the human experience, in a state of acceptance of *what is*.

Learning to arrive is all about training the mind.

Our minds can get *so* ahead of us. I used to get ahead of

myself *a lot*. I used to worry about my future, worry about my family, worry about whether I was going to make it. I played out every single possible scenario. This is really what anxiety is: a state of worrying about the future and being too sped up and stressed out to arrive in the now.

Our minds can also have an addiction to replaying the past. You may relive every conversation you had with a particular person or analyze how you could have done something differently years ago. Memories and feelings of guilt, resentment, bitterness, and sadness entangle your mind and keep it from arriving in the now.

On both sides, trouble arises from missing the present moment. When you try to speed up to the future, you get stress and anxiety. When you replay the past, you get resentment and regret. (And when you seesaw between both of those, which certainly happens, you get emotional whiplash.)

It may not seem like you have complete control of your mind. But you actually do! And your practice of being aware of your thoughts will directly correlate with your arrival in the present moment — and the enjoyment and peace you will experience as you arrive.

Realize that there is nowhere for you to go, nothing you need to say, nothing you need to do. Release the past and let go of the future. All you get to do is just be right here, right now, and experience all the release that's possible when you surrender into your being — *the beingness of you.*

"That's great, Jolie," you might be thinking now, "but how do I actually *do* this?"

I want to answer that with a quote from Marianne Williamson's book *A Return to Love*. It reads: "We can act and think out of fear, or we can act and think out of love." The easiest way to learn to arrive is to examine our thoughts from this perspective. Are we thinking, planning, speaking, or acting out of fear or out of love? I promise you that one of these allows you to arrive in the present moment and the other does not.

Fear is what focuses us on the past. Fear is what fixates us on the future. Fear is what tells us that the present moment has no value. Fear is what keeps us grabbing for the next thing even when we know we have all we need right now. And when we fill up our brain bandwidth with jealousy, comparison, resentment, regret, and competition, it will always bring us into fear and out of the present moment.

Simply asking whether a thought comes from love or from fear is a powerful step in the art of arrival.

Here are some other steps I love:

- **SLOW DOWN.** Imagine yourself in all the arenas of your life, effortlessly gliding from scene to scene. Whatever you do, give yourself a bit of extra time to do it slowly and consciously. (This is particularly helpful in the car!)

- **BE AWARE OF PEOPLE YOU HABITUALLY MIMIC.** My mom was always in a rush. She was perpetually five minutes late, throwing things in the car, weaving in and out of traffic, always in a "go go go" mode. So guess what I would always do without even thinking about it? Are you mimicking someone else's pace to fit in? Can you think of more present, arrived role models to follow?

- **BREATHE!** Give yourself nice, big inhales, feeling the oxygen fill up your body, and exhale to release everything that's not serving you. Breath work practices are a key to accessing presence. Yoga

and meditation can help you feel your breath even
more deeply.

- LISTEN. Have you ever had a friend truly listen to
you? It's a gift we take for granted. But so many of
us aren't truly listening to the people we converse
with. We always have this mental chatter going on
in the background saying, "I already know what
they're going to say. What they're saying isn't important. I want to prepare what I'm going to say
next." Stop thinking and listen to them! Practicing
listening will ensure that you are present.

- EAT WITH PRESENCE. When meals arrive, many
of us just think, "Nom nom nom, get in my belly."
But to be in the present moment, allow yourself
to be excited by the visuals, take in the smells and
tastes and textures, say a quick blessing for the
food. Chew slowly and swallow deliberately. You'll
be amazed at how much better your body is able to
digest the food and how this practice puts you in a
space of gratitude and presence.

The world needs more people who are willing to fully
arrive, to fully be in the here and now. Are you willing to be
one? Can you promise yourself to slow down, remember the
uniqueness and beauty of you, let go of the future and the past,
and access the state of ease, grace, and lightness that's waiting
for you? Everything you want is already *right here*.

Allow yourself to arrive.

At this point in our process together, we have done a lot
of inner work. We have looked at how you relate to yourself,
how you relate to others, and how you relate to the divine.
You've done a great job staying with the process up until this

point! I am so proud of you, sister. I know this has been a lot to digest.

As you invite more presence into your life, I want you to literally stop and smell the roses. I want you to have the juiciest, sexiest, most pleasurable life. Don't miss the little things. Paradise is all around you to enjoy if you give yourself the gift of presence.

In the next chapter, I am going to share with you the secrets to manifesting anything that you want to create in your life. Now that you have the strong foundation of Self, it's time to go out there into the world, create some magic, and have some fun!

CHAPTER TWELVE

I Am a Manifesting Queen

I used to watch in awe as the people around me created seemingly nonstop epic shit: exotic vacations, exclusive parties with celebrities, six-figure businesses, random free gifts — you name it, they created it, and social media was the deliverer of the constant message. I always wondered how the heck they did it. How was it that some of my friends understood how to create anything they wanted and others — like me — just wished for it?

Before long, I started to hear about this buzzword, *manifesting*. You've probably heard it, too — it gets tossed around a lot in life coaching and personal development circles. When I first heard it, it sounded like magic: you say that you're manifesting something, and then, *poof*, it shows up. But at that point, it seemed way too good to me to be true. Is that really how it works?

Actually, yes. Manifesting does work that way — and it does *work*. But there's a bit more to understand about it in order to achieve the desired effect.

Let's start with the word itself. *Manifest* means to be evidence of something, to prove it. So what you're doing when you manifest is bringing the evidence of something you desire into your life and reality, which allows the thing itself to show up.

Remember that everything you want to be, you already are. So any possible goal or vision that you can imagine is already yours. This knowledge is the key to manifesting.

It definitely doesn't feel that easy when your bank account balance is in the red and you have rent to pay. That shit feels very real. But let me assure you, money is all around you, in an infinite supply. You just have to be willing to reach down and pick it up! And money is just the beginning of what you can manifest.

So what is it that you want in your life? More money, a nicer wardrobe, a job you love, to make an impact in the world, to find your true love, to create harmony in your family? Are you ready to receive those things? Let's dive in.

Seven Steps to Turn On Your Manifesting Superpowers

I'm going to share with you the seven steps I use to manifest prosperity, success, and tangible miracles in my life. I first discovered these steps through work with Darryl Anka and the being he channels, Bashar, and I've expanded on them for further clarity as I've used them. (Note: as you read through these, you'll notice some similarities to the law of attraction work we explored earlier. This is intentional! Manifesting is a more active and in-depth exploration of that law.)

1. *Visualize*

You must be able to see what you want, and you must be able to see yourself having it.

Many people say that they would love a million dollars. They can see what a million dollars looks like: a nice car, shopping trips, travel, et cetera. But they don't see themselves having it. It's always someone else in the vision.

The way to visualize is to put *you* in the frame. You're depositing the check, you've got the cash in your hands, and you're paying for the house/car/trip with that cash. If you want a romantic relationship in your life, visualize yourself going on dates with that person. Imagine them buying you flowers, opening the car door for you, and so on.

Guided meditations for visualization can be very helpful here. These meditations verbally lead you into invoking your imagination and seeing your desires clearly in your mind's eye. If you aren't sure how to start this step or would like some guidance, this kind of meditation tool can be a great help.

2. *Desire*

The thing you desire isn't just something that would be kind of nice to have, maybe, if it works out, someday. The thing you want has to come with strong emotion — you must *really, really want it*. This intensity gives your desire energy. The more strongly and intensely you're able to create the emotion around the desire, the more easily you will attract it into your experience.

I love to build intense emotion around my desire to travel the world. I create pinboards of all the places I want to go. Right now, for instance, I have a whole board dedicated to Thailand

and East Asia. As I see the pictures on it, I allow myself to develop joy, excitement, thrill, and wonderment around wanting to go there. I imagine myself lying on a beautiful massage table and getting a massage by the ocean as I hear the waves roll up around me. I invoke the feelings of relaxation, gratitude, surrender, and divine appreciation and let them wash over me.

Try doing this for fifteen minutes. Pick something you desire and allow yourself to get totally moved by the thing that you are calling in. Energize your emotions around it, turn that energy up, and then expand it. Have fun with it! You actually get to experience the joy of a future moment right now if you allow yourself to have it. It's pretty amazing. And when you combine the ability to create a future that turns you on with a practice of presence and full acceptance of the now, you strike the perfect balance of creation and surrender.

3. Believe

As with the law of attraction, you must believe that it is possible, even inevitable, for *you* to manifest the thing you want.

The big mistake that people made when they read *The Secret* or watched the film was that they simply wrote themselves an imaginary $10 million check and then just hoped that it would come to them. Many who did this still held an underlying belief that they couldn't have it, that they didn't deserve it, that it would come for other people but not them. They didn't take the time and invest the effort in believing that *they* could have the check. So of course it never actually showed up for them.

Your strongest belief always wins.

In order to manifest, you must believe that you are capable of manifesting. So begin where you are. Start with something that you can actually believe yourself manifesting *right now*. Maybe you don't jump right to owning the beach house. Maybe you start with manifesting enough additional income to be able to rent a place near the ocean. That's perfectly okay. Starting small gives you experience, which in turn breeds confidence in your ability to manifest larger and larger things.

4. Accept

Doubt is a manifestation killer. You must totally accept the new vision of yourself and your new belief in your ability to manifest, beyond a shadow of doubt. Be very matter-of-fact with your goals and dreams. Accept them as the truth right now, as this is the only moment that ever exists. You need not try to convince others of the truth, but be confident and commanding in your acceptance within and for yourself. This puts you in the space of nonresistance.

It is important here that you understand the old belief systems you have that may conflict with your new (or newly defined) desire.

For instance, if you say you want your business to make $10,000 a month but the stronger belief you hold is that money is the root of all evil, then you are in resistance, not acceptance. You must be aware of what you're resisting in order to change it and start accepting new beliefs.

5. Intend

Intending to have something is different from wanting it. You can be in the space of wanting for your entire life and never receive the pleasure of experiencing having what you want. Intention is taking your desire to the level of consciousness and command. You know that your world is created by your word. You trust yourself to command your own experience. So you state the intention to have your experience include the things you desire.

For example, here's a recent intention I have set for myself: I am going to use my voice in the world to assist in the awakening of my generation. I see myself speaking on big stages, not because my ego wants me to be famous, but because I know I have a big mission in the world.

So I use my intention to call in the experiences that I need to get me there. I don't sit around saying, "Oh, that would be nice someday, whenever it gets to me." No, I wake up every day with an intention to be my best Self, to call in experiences that prep me to speak at that level, and to command my experience rather than waiting for someone else to create it for me.

6. Act

Next, you must act as if you currently have the thing that you're calling in. Behave as if it already exists, make the space in your life for it, carry yourself as if you have it.

Arielle Ford, a relationship expert, has spoken many times about making room in your life to attract your soul mate to enter. She recommends actions like making room in the closet for their clothes, removing pictures of former lovers from your walls and desk, going out to celebrate your new love, buying tickets for two to an event a few months in advance. With this level of action, you are trusting yourself to create your desires. This trust is incredibly powerful. You can use it to start magnetizing the energy you want to find you faster.

Similarly, if you are wanting to attract more money, start carrying yourself as if you have $5,000 in cash in your wallet and your private jet is picking you and your friends up this afternoon. Go inside a high-end store and believe yourself to be worthy of having everything there.

Allow yourself to feel the pleasure of having it all now, with no resistance, no feeling sorry for yourself, no guilt, and no doubting the experience.

7. *Release*

Okay. Now that you know exactly what you want and how you would like to feel having it, it's time to let it go. You must completely detach from the outcome. Trust the work you've done so far to meet your needs and desires, and trust the master plan of the universe to unfold with grace. Surrender your need to control how that will happen.

Sometimes the thing that you ask for will show up in a completely different way than you expect. You can't see the entire story, and you don't need to see it or understand the how. What we think we desire and what we actually want may be completely different, and time will reveal that.

This is the trickiest step, not just because surrender is difficult when we're so used to controlling everything, but also because we may have been so focused on a particular desire that we missed other ways the universe could bless us. To receive the full blessing of the manifestation experience, we must be willing to surrender even the thing we started out wanting to manifest.

That sounds contradictory, but I promise it isn't.

Think about it this way: When the Buddha talks about letting go of desire, he doesn't mean we should stop wanting things. He means we should stop wishing we were somewhere other than where we are now. When you surrender your desire to change your current state of being, you gain the ability to call in abundance to that current state.

So are you willing to have what you want where you are right now? I invite you to explore your own willingness. Start by practicing the manifestation process outlined above. What could show up right now that would make all the difference for you? Start with something that you believe you can have, even if it's as small as manifesting a good parking spot. Then move up from there. You are more powerful than you know. Play with your power. Have fun with it. You'll love the results.

Manifesting Your Purpose in This Life

I suggest above that you start small, but once you get comfortable with manifesting, you can go big...or start going big *right now*, because you *can* manifest your purpose in this life, and you *can* manifest it now. Why waste any more time wondering why you're here?

This is what I did. Here's my story of manifesting my purpose.

After college, I didn't know what the heck I was going to do.

Nothing seemed like a fit. The first business I started failed, and I didn't trust myself to start another one. I knew I was good in sales and good at working with people, so, following a friend's advice, I got my real estate broker's license.

The problem was, although studying for the license had given me some much-needed direction, I knew that it wasn't right for me almost as soon as I got it. Working in real estate did not speak to me, inspire me, or excite me, but I stuck it out because I wanted to appear as if I had it all together. (Remember the pretending game that I had gotten so good at? Yeah, that was still going full force.)

So I got a job at a real estate investment company. As jobs go, it was a great one. I worked out of an office on a multimillion-dollar La Jolla estate, spent only four hours a day in the office, left whenever I wanted to, and was paid a salary. I tried to focus on all the perks to make up for not really wanting to be there, but I still wasn't fulfilled. I knew real estate work wasn't my purpose or my greatest contribution in the world. On some level, I knew I wanted to lead people, to start movements, to do something *greater* than hustle real estate investments.

But I was also afraid to pursue those things. After my first business failed, I unknowingly bought into a very common conversation around both the real estate industry and life in general: women aren't meant to be leaders. No matter how much I wanted to lead, I told myself I just wasn't fit for it. This turmoil even showed up in my romantic relationship. Since my perceived role was to take care of the home and support my man in achieving something great rather than achieving it myself, I was putting *major* marriage pressure on my partner, even as I tried to cram my big dreams into his shadow.

This tug-of-war between big dreams and oppressive fears was not fun. In fact, it pretty much sucked. But I didn't know how to get out of it by myself!

I ended up taking a three-month coaching course on leadership and self-expression. Everyone in the course was challenged to take on a project. It had to be something that impacted the community as a whole, that had measurable results, and that could be completed in three months — and we had to lead it by ourselves.

This assignment changed the course of my career forever.

For the first time in my life, I was given the space to completely make up whatever I wanted to do. I finally had permission to look within and access my truest desires. Since I was going through a pretty big spiritual transformation at the time, I decided I wanted to start a conversation with other women my age about awakening, breaking out of the illusion of this reality, remembering our inherent divinity, and acknowledging daily miracles.

I hosted a free event for young women called Inner Goddess Unleashed. I ended up having seven speakers, more than $2,000 worth of sponsored food, drinks, and goodies, and eighty-five attendees.

I remember the moment when I really absorbed the results that were happening around me because of my deliberate action. With no drive other than a simple assignment and my own passion, I had created an event that impacted more than eighty of my peers. In that moment, I knew for the first time that I could lead. It was like I tapped into an unlimited reservoir of power and energy that I'd never found in myself before. It was one of the most powerful moments of my life.

I quit my job in real estate, and I never went back to a corporate job. Two years later, my events hosted hundreds of women, with *New York Times* bestselling authors coming to speak and making a massive contribution. When I was twenty-five, *Pacific* magazine named me as one of San Diego's top thirty under thirty entrepreneurs. Creating and leading these events inspired me to launch my now wildly successful coaching company, Prosperity Queendom Inc. Alongside my team, I created the largest women's money meditation challenge on the internet, called Dare to Prosper. Thousands of women around the globe have been transformed by my leadership and teachings. Many days, it's a challenge for me to receive all the gratitude and appreciation that flow to me. Every single time I launch a course (which is many times per year), I create multi–six figures of income. *Entrepreneur* magazine accepted me as a contributing author, and I have six bestselling books on Amazon. I travel often, treat myself to world-class experiences, take epic care of my body, and enjoy freedom of choice. Most importantly, I feel empowered every day because I created this life by doing something I love — something I'd do even if I weren't being paid.

This is the power of manifestation rituals. And it's also what purpose feels like.

So what does it really mean to live on purpose?

Living on Purpose

The word *purpose* is defined by Lexico.com as "the reason for which something is done or created or for which something exists."

In essence, your purpose is the reason that you exist. It is *why* you took birth, *why* you wanted to be in a human body, and *why* you feel driven to do something great. You manifested *yourself* on this earth to fulfill a purpose. That's profound! Living with purpose means that each of us is ultimately the creator of our own experience. The world is your blank canvas, and you are the one holding the paintbrush.

We tend to make purpose harder than it needs to be; we imagine we need to go out into the world and make it happen, like there is something to do or figure out. But remember, you don't need to know the how. Trying to find your purpose outside of yourself is like searching for the glasses that are on top of your head. It's fruitless to look outside; you'll only find it when you're willing to look at what you already have. Your purpose is within you.

Do you feel like you know why you're here?

If you're like most of our generation of millennials, you may feel like you want something more but don't know how to create it. The millennials get a bad rap. Apparently we are overly obsessed with ourselves, noncommittal, and defiant. What if we are just hypercurious and aware that something other than what we've been taught is possible? Maybe we just aren't willing to subscribe to the whole work-to-the-bone-to-get-what-you-want attitude. Maybe we just want to live with purpose!

This generation is different from any other generation. We see the smashing success of companies like TOMS Shoes, Whole Foods Market, lululemon, and brands that have a greater *why* behind them than just financial gain. The people who run these companies want to know that what they are doing actually makes a difference.

Our generation is seeking the *why* more than ever, and that's all you need to know to manifest your purpose. Why does the why matter to us? Because we are waking up as a species. We're starting to see that following what our parents and their parents did isn't the only way to live. We are noticing that there is another way, that we don't have to push so hard, and that we don't have to sacrifice just to get by. We are recognizing that love, money, and status don't have to be a big scary deal and that finding our purposes can empower us to shine our unique brilliance, impact the world, and live lives that turn us on.

Here are five steps I've learned along the way that will help you really do the thing that lights you up most in the world. If you know what you want to do and be, these steps will help you get there. And if you don't, they'll help you find it.

1. *The World Is Your Playground*

Please remember that you are here on planet Earth because you wanted the experience of creating in the physical realm. Are you enjoying your physical experience? Or do you want to create more?

Starting a business is one of the most beautiful arenas of creation you can play in. The word *business* has so many associations attached to it, but it simply means "busy-ness," aka that thing that keeps you busy. So what do you want to be busy with? If you allow yourself to have fun with it and keep "playing" instead of "working," then you will be able to fuel your creative passion instead of getting burned out. (And if anyone wants to take on renaming the notion of "business" to be lighter and more appealing, I will totally be behind you on that.)

So what would *you* do if you could do anything? And what will it take for you to believe that your desire can become a possibility?

What I've found is that everyone knows on some level what they really love doing and what they would love to get paid for. They just haven't felt the permission to go for it. What if you granted yourself permission right now? To have what you truly want? To move boldly toward your dreams?

Something very curious starts to happen when you choose for yourself and believe in your chosen destiny. Doors open, miracles happen, and support shows up out of nowhere. This is the universe confirming that you are on the right path and rewarding you for following your heart.

2. *Make Shit Up*

Are you willing to try?

Seriously, I know it looks like Richard Branson knows what

he's doing, but he's literally making it up as he goes along. Did Elon Musk have any idea how to create an electric car company? Nope, he followed his passion and took a stand to disrupt an industry. Those guys were enjoying their time on the playground, and they believed their passions were important, just as any kid knows, without ever being told, how important it is to *play*. You can do this, too.

Don't get me wrong: it's essential to educate yourself with skills and actually have the right tools. But when it comes to jumping in and creating, just say *yes* and then figure out how to do it as you go. You can Google anything now, so there are no excuses anymore to say, "I don't know how."

A friend I met at an entrepreneurship festival saw that I had bought an in-home production studio and was recording content. She asked me if I could help her shoot her application video for *Shark Tank*. I immediately said yes and explained to her how I would help her direct the shoot. I'd never done that before, I had no previous experience, I totally made that shit up. Then I figured it out. I went on YouTube to learn lighting and sound. I asked for advice from friends who knew more than me. And I was persistent, learning through a lot of trial and error. But I believed in myself, and I trusted that I had everything I needed to do an awesome job for her. And it happened. I manifested it.

You can totally make shit up the exact same way. Play, then watch your game come true and change your life into what you always dreamed it could be. You'll never get bored, and you'll always love what you do.

3. When You Believe in Yourself, Others Will, Too

A funny thing happens when you start a new business or project. You make something up, like "I'm a jewelry designer" or

"I'm a copywriter." When you actually start producing results, you say to yourself, "Hey, I'm kind of good at this." Then, when you get a big win with a client or start seeing lots of sales with your jewelry or copywriting, you say, "Hey, I'm really good at this. I believe in myself even more." Eventually, you will believe at the deepest level that you really are a jewelry designer or a copywriter, and it won't be long before the world sees it and believes it, too, because that's exactly what you've become. Passion + belief = manifestation.

The more you believe in you, the more other people believe you. It's that simple. Then, when you get to a Tony Robbins level and you have epic confidence in yourself and your abilities, people will pay you $1 million a year to work with you — not just because your skills are exactly what they need, but also because *they deeply want to believe in themselves at the level you do*. They want to know how you did it.

4. Pick One Thing to Start

What if the issue isn't that you don't believe you can start but that you don't know which thing to start with? Sometimes there are so many options that you can't make up your mind! I've heard this from several clients. They say, "I could start a yoga company or a vegan cupcake shop or a relationship course, or I could join a multi-level marketing scheme that my friends have been raving about, or I could become a blogger."

And then they don't start any of them.

You must pick *one* thing. Period.

Other things can come later. For right now, pick one and only one. Don't let your focus become diluted. Concentrate it all in one spot. For now.

If you have multiple directions available to you, make a list of them all. Lay the list out in front of you. Go through your options one by one and visualize the best-case scenario for each of them. What would it look like if you reached ulti- mate success in this or that path? Now, which one is the most exciting to you? Which one makes you giddy like a child on Christmas? Got one? Good!

If you're having a hard time with this exercise, consider that you may be addicted to the cop-out of pretending that you don't know what you want so that you don't have to make any choices. Face that excuse and pick one anyway!

5. Jump In

Now get started! Seriously, stop kicking the can around, pre- tending like you don't know what to do. You are here because you deeply desire to uncover your true purpose. You just made the choice of what you're going to start. All that remains is for you to jump in and see what you can accomplish.

What is one thing you can do today to get started? Find that thing and then do it. Every tiny action gets you closer to the big picture. When you begin saying yes to the thing that lights your soul up, all the invisible forces align and start work- ing for you. Trust in your divine path. Choose it. Say yes and keep taking action, and your dream will materialize before your eyes.

Whether you decide to start a side project, launch a new business, expand what you've already created, or just commit yourself to being a more positive person in the world, you now have all the tools that you need to be able to do it. You can have and be and do anything you want. Remember, you took birth here to experience new things and have fun! You've got this, sister!

CONCLUSION

I Am Empowered, Sexy,

and Free

So here we are, at the end of the journey together. Divine, radiant, woman, I am so honored that you made it this far. I am very aware that some of the sections of this book can be very confronting, bring up all kinds of feeling and emotional memories, and can even make you question everything you know about this reality. I am so grateful that you held space for my vulnerability and listened to my stories. I do not take it lightly that you spent your precious time with this book.

What I've shown you here is the foundation for continual integration and practice. I invite you to keep up your journaling practice, remain aware of reining in your ego so it continues to work with you instead of against you, keep your awareness on your triggers, and embrace your soul contracts. This book contains a lot of juicy information, the kind that I wish I had discovered when I was early on my awakening path, and it's great to be inspired, but it's only life changing when you're willing to put the ideas into practice.

In the subtitle of this book, I promised to deliver you the knowledge to discover your unique brilliance and dare to be the creatrix of your life. I set out to divulge the formula to having a life that totally turns you on. I thought I would save the crux of this for last.

What do I mean by a life that turns you on? I don't mean it in a sexual way, although that's an element of it. When I look at my life, I feel my whole body scream a *yes*! I absolutely love traveling the world, I've got a kick-ass community of loving, conscious friends, and I have lots of intentional beauty around me.

A life that turns you on means that you feel activated by your life, you love what you've created, you're proud of your hard work, and you continually have the courage to ask for more. I truly believe the world will change entirely when women reclaim their power and move from the autopilot life to the life of leadership and initiative that so many of us have forgotten we have access to.

You will be able to feel it in your body when you are living that yes to your life. You will feel expanded, light, free, and turned *on*.

Now that you know how to manifest anything you desire, now that you know how to create harmony in your relationships, and now that you know how to have mastery over your emotions through self-processing and journaling, the world is your oyster. The things that used to hold you back are simply not a problem anymore. You have a full toolbox to help you move beyond them. That junk that was covering the brilliance of you has been lifted. All opportunities are available to you. Allow yourself to be turned on by your life. Allow spontaneous moments of ecstasy and orgasmic pleasure to arise in your body just by remembering how much you love being alive. Be your favorite person to come home to.

I hereby grant you the permission to feel an entirely new capacity for prosperity and pleasure, to unapologetically love yourself and your life, and to inspire everyone around you with your contagious joy.

I grant you permission to express yourself in any ridiculous, crazy, wild way that you would like. To give your gift of happiness to the world and leave a legacy that outlives your physical body.

I grant you the pleasure of remembering that *you* are the only one who can grant yourself anything.

I hold up the mirror of remembrance for you to realize that you never needed me in the first place to grant you permission for anything. That was always your power, and I just happen to be the one to reflect it back to you.

We all leave a legacy based on how we have lived and what we have done. What will your legacy be? It can be broad and bright and full of joy. Your legacy can be:

- the spiritual light inside you that you chose to nurture
- the inner child whom you rescued from her past
- the sexual innocence and power that you reclaimed as yours
- the garden of purpose that you nurtured for years and tended to from deep within your soul
- the prosperity that flowed out of you like a Hawaiian waterfall
- the time you took to know yourself as truth, so you could be the example of light for others

You can leave a mark by living with passion, manifesting your purpose, and being everything you have been dreaming that you might one day be. You can start right now; the world is at your feet, and your heart is the compass. What will you do, beautiful friend, with the rest of your time here on this beautiful planet? The answer is in you, and I can't wait to see what happens when you bring it into the light.

Right now, we are creating the future. We are determining whether our planet lives in love or in fear, in expansion or in contraction, in bliss or in pain. The choice is yours. Make it sexy.

Say it with me:

I am Empowered.

I am Sexy.

I am Free.

And so it is.

Acknowledgments

To the great thinkers listed below, who paved the way for a conversation about awakening and personal development that has greatly impacted my life, entrepreneurship journey, and spiritual path: Thank you for your books, theories, methods, and transmissions.

Oprah Winfrey (creator of *Super Soul Sunday*)
Dale Carnegie (author of *How to Win Friends and Influence People*)
Alan Watts (creator of *You're It*)
Esther Hicks (thought leader on the law of attraction)
Richard Rudd (author of *The Gene Keys*)
Napoleon Hill (author of *Think and Grow Rich*)
Arturo Gaitan (creator of Transmutation Meditation)
Marianne Williamson (author of *A Return to Love*)
Werner Erhard (original creator of the technology behind Landmark Worldwide)
Tony Robbins (creator of *Unleash the Power Within*)

Gabrielle Bernstein (author of *Spirit Junkie*)
Paulo Coelho (author of *The Alchemist*)
Timothy Ferriss (author of *The 4-Hour Workweek*)
Eckhart Tolle (author of *The Power of Now*)
Neale Donald Walsch (author of *Conversations with God*)
Richard Branson (prolific entrepreneur and creator of the Virgin brand)
Peter H. Diamandis (coauthor of *Abundance*)
Marie Forleo (creator of *MarieTV*)
Cory Michelle (creator of the 5D Creation Process)

To all the women who are choosing the path of awakening: Thank you for being kind to yourself, for making empowered choices for your lives, for being part of the great awakening on the planet. Your feminine heart and empathy point the way to a better future for all of us. Your love, your leadership, and your creative essence inspire me greatly. Thank you for being here, in this crazy human experience with me.

To my friends and soul sisters who have loved me through my blossoming: You've had my back, supported me, and stayed by my side in times of trial. Because of you, I know what true sisterhood feels like. We've grown beyond the old paradigm of competition, comparison, judgment, and gossip. Instead, we celebrate one another, acknowledge one another, and hold the highest vision of light for one another. I feel like the wealthiest woman in the world because of all my beautiful sister connections. I am so grateful for you — thank you for being by my side on this journey.

To my birth family, Lynn, Walter, and Tres Pinkerton: Thank you for being the exact soul contracts that I needed in this lifetime to allow me to grow into the woman I am. Mom, Dad, your love is never forgotten and lives through my legacy. Brother, you and I have been through so much. Thank you for always being by my side and cheering me on. You're truly the best.

About the
Author

Jolie Dawn is the creator of the Dare to Prosper Challenge, the largest women's prosperity meditation gathering online, attended by women in more than fifty countries. She specializes in helping women awaken their prosperity consciousness, embody their deepest truth, and reclaim personal freedom and creativity. An intuitive business coach and writer, she currently contributes to *Entrepreneur* magazine, and she has written six bestselling self-published books, including *The Empowered Woman Series* and *The Spiritual Journey of Entrepreneurship*. She is the founder of Prosperity Queendom Inc., an online business-training platform for spiritual entrepreneurs. Jolie has had thousands of hours of leadership and spirituality training in various modalities, including hypnosis, unconscious reprogramming, Kundalini yoga, ThetaHealing, Reiki, and transmutation meditation. She currently lives in Hawaii.

You can access all the bonus exercises that accompany this book at joliedawn.com/esf as well as learn about Jolie's offerings at joliedawn.com. She is also active on Instagram with the handle @joliedawnxo.